Depth St

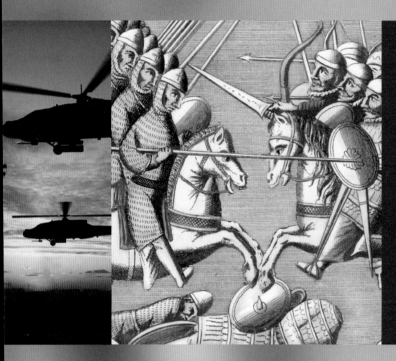

Warfare
The Changing Face of Armed Conflict

Aaron Wilkes

OXFORD
UNIVERSITY PRESS

OXFORD
UNIVERSITY PRESS

Great Clarendon Street, Oxford OX2 6DP

Oxford University Press is a department of the University of Oxford.

It furthers the University's objective of excellence in research, scholarship, and education by publishing worldwide in Oxford

New York   Auckland   Cape Town   Dar es Salaam   Hong Kong
Karachi   Kuala Lumpur   Madrid   Melbourne   Mexico City
Nairobi   New Delhi   Shanghai   Taipei   Toronto

With offices in

Argentina   Austria   Brazil   Chile   Czech Republic   France   Greece
Guatemala   Hungary   Italy   Japan   Poland   Portugal   Singapore
South Korea   Switzerland   Thailand   Turkey   Ukraine   Vietnam

Oxford is a registered trade mark of Oxford University Press
in the UK and in certain other countries

© Aaron Wilkes 2011

The moral rights of the authors have been asserted

Database right Oxford University Press (maker)

First published 2011

All rights reserved. No part of this publication may be reproduced, stored in a retrieval system, or transmitted, in any form or by any means, without the prior permission in writing of Oxford University Press, or as expressly permitted by law, or under terms agreed with the appropriate reprographics rights organization. Enquiries concerning reproduction outside the scope of the above should be sent to the Rights Department, Oxford University Press, at the address above

You must not circulate this book in any other binding or cover and you must impose this same condition on any acquirer

British Library Cataloguing in Publication Data

Data available

ISBN 978-1-85008-557-7

10 9 8 7 6 5 4 3 2

Printed in Singapore by KHL Printing Co Pte Ltd

Acknowledgements

Text design and layouts: Sally Boothroyd

Illustrators: Tony Randell and Clive Wakfer

Cover Images: TebNad/Shutterstock, Bettmann/CORBIS, koh sze kiat/Shutterstock

The publisher would like to thank the following for permission to reproduce photographs:

Christopher Furlong/Getty Images: P6; Keystone/Getty Images: P7; Hulton-Deutsch Collection/Corbis: P7; Fox Photos/Getty Images: P8; Aaron Wilkes: P8; Richard Klune/Corbis: P8; Mary Evans Picture Library/Rue Des Archives: P9; Mary Evans/Rue des Archives/Tallandier: P12; Time & Life Pictures/Getty Images: P12; Gamma-Keystone/Getty Images: P13; Mary Evans Picture Library: P14; Mary Evans Picture Library: P15; Reuters/Corbis: P15; Skyscan/Corbis: P15; Aaron Allmon II/U.S. Air Force/Reuters/Corbis: P15; Time & Life Pictures/Getty Images: P16; Spencer Platt/Getty Images: P16; Mary Evans Picture Library: P17; Mary Evans Picture Library: P17; Holton Collection/Getty Images: P18; Mary Evans Picture Library: P19; Mary Evans Picture Library: P19; Mary Evans Picture Library: P22; AFP/ Getty Images: P24; Scott Rothstein/Shutterstock: P25; Hulton-Deutsch Collection/CORBIS: P25; Corbis: P25; United States Navy: P26; Fox Photos/Getty Images: P27; Mary Evans Picture Library: P29; Roger Viollet/Getty Images: P30; Bettmann/CORBIS: P32; Popperfoto/Getty Images: P33; CORBIS: P48; Photoquest/Getty Images: P48; Skyscan/CORBIS: P49; Skyscan/Corbis: P49; Mary Evans/Roger Worsley Archive: P50; Suddeutsche Zeitung/Mary Evans Picture Library: P50; Hulton-Deutsch Collection/CORBIS: P50; CORBIS: P50; Mary Evans/Robert Hunt Collection: P51; Popperfoto/Getty Images: P51; Hulton Archive/Getty Images: P51; Galerie Bilderwelt/Getty Images: P51; CORBIS: P58; AFP/Getty Images: P59.

Aaron Wilkes wishes to thank Sarah Flynn/Rebecca Bernard of OUP, as well as Kate Redmond, for all their hard work and advice.

The author and publisher are grateful for permission to reprint extracts from the following copyright material:

Margaret G Arnstein: 'Florence Nightingale's Influence on Nursing', *Bulletin of the New York Academy of Medicine*, V 32, No 7, July 1956, reprinted by permission of the New York Academy of Medicine.

Brian Brady and Jonathan Owen: 'Revealed: £12bn hidden costs of Afghan War', *The Independent*, 26.7.2009, copyright © The Independent 2009, reprinted by permission of The Independent.

Nigel Kelly and Rosemary Rees: *The Modern World* (Heinemann, 1996), reprinted by permission of Pearson Education Ltd.

Peter Moss: *History Alive 1, 1485-1714* (Hart Davis Educational, 1975) and *History Alive 4, 1900-1970s* (Hart Davis Educational, 1977), reprinted by permission of Pearson Education Ltd.

Gerri Peev: 'UK's £20 bn bill for fighting Iraq and Afghan Wars', *Daily Mail*, 21.6.2010, reprinted by permission of Solo Syndication.

Peace Pledge Union: from web page at www.ppu.org.uk, reprinted by permission of the Peace Pledge Union.

Although we have made every effort to trace and contact all copyright holders before publication this has not been possible in all cases. If notified, the publisher
will rectify any errors or omissions at the earliest opportunity.

The websites recommended in this publication were correct at the time of going to press; however, websites may have been removed or web addresses changed since that time. OUP has made every attempt to suggest websites that are reliable and appropriate for students' use. It is not unknown for unscrupulous individuals to put unsuitable material on websites that may be accessed by students. Teachers should check all websites before allowing students to access them. OUP is not responsible for the content of external websites.

Contents

What is history?

Before you start this book, take a few minutes to think about these questions.

- What do you think history is? What does the word mean?
- What have you learnt in history lessons before, perhaps in your primary school or in other years at secondary school? Did you enjoy your history lessons or not? If you enjoyed them, say why. If you didn't enjoy them, why not?
- Have you read any history books or stories about things that happened a long time ago? Have you watched any television programmes, films or plays about things that happened in the past? If so, which ones?
- Can you remember any wars or battles that you might have studied?

History is about what happened in the past. It is about people in the past, what they did and why they did it, what they thought and what they felt. To enjoy history you need to have a good imagination. You need to be able to imagine what life was like in the past, or what it may have been like to be involved in past events.

How did people feel, think and react to events like these?

It's June 1645 and I'm a soldier in the New Model Army, fighting in the English Civil War. We're the country's first full-time professional army. Training is tough, but at least it's an army based on ability rather than position in society. If you're a good enough soldier, you'll go far! I'm a musketeer – I have a long gun that uses gunpowder to fire metal balls at the enemy. Guns are quite a new weapon – I wonder if they're here to stay? Will they replace swords, clubs and pikes? And what other new weapons will there be in the future?

It's July 1917 and I'm worried sick. My husband is away fighting in France and I haven't heard from him for ages. We pray for his safe return every night. Enemy ships have shelled towns on the coast and planes have bombed London. Millions of men are away fighting and we women are doing their jobs in the factories and on farms. I wonder if we'll be allowed to carry on working when the men come home? I believe our government when they say we'll win this war... but will it really be the war to end all wars?

It's February 2003 and I'm protesting against yet another war. Will countries never learn that war is just wrong? It's brutal, bloody, cruel, destructive... and very expensive. Politicians start wars, but it's the young people who fight and die in them. And there are never any real winners in war – only losers. So why do nations keep fighting them? It's crazy! In my opinion, war can never be justified in any circumstances... can it?

How to use this book

As you work through this book, you will notice a number of features that keep appearing.

MISSION OBJECTIVES

MISSION ACCOMPLISHED?

All sections of this book will start by setting your Mission Objectives. These are your key aims that set out your learning targets for the work ahead. Topics will end by trying to get you to assess your own learning. If you can accomplish each Mission Objective then you are doing well!

WISE-UP Words are key terms that are vital to help you discuss and understand the topics. You can spot them easily because they are in bold type. Look up their meanings in a dictionary or use the Glossary at the end of the book. The Glossary is a list of words and their meanings.

Some topics contain PAUSE for Thought boxes. This is an opportunity for you to stop and think for yourself.

 Hungry for MORE

The Hungry for MORE features give you a chance to extend your knowledge and research beyond the classroom. This is a time for you to take responsibility for your own learning. You might be asked to research something in the library or on the Internet, work on a presentation, or design and make something. Can you meet the challenge?

 FACT

These are all the fascinating, amazing or astounding little bits of history that you usually don't get to hear about! But we think they are just as important and give you insights into topics that you'll easily remember.

 BIG QUESTION

This book will ask you to consider some of the 'Big Questions' about war and warfare. You will be encouraged to think about why wars happen, how they have changed over the centuries, how much they cost and whether or not they can ever be justified.

 **DEPTH STUDY**

There are also three Depth Studies in this book. These will get you to focus on the following themes:

- **WEAPONS OF WAR**
- **WAR AND MEDICINE**
- **THE WORLD AT WAR**

These Depth Studies focus on the methods used in war and the impact war has had on people and technology throughout history.

 Work

Work sections are your opportunity to demonstrate your knowledge and understanding.
You might be asked to:
- put events in the correct chronological order
- explain how things have changed over time
- work out why two people might interpret the same event differently
- work out what triggered an event to take place in the short term or the long term
- compare, contrast, categorise, summarise, judge, justify, criticise or assess.

Why do we study war and warfare?

─────────────── MISSION OBJECTIVES ───────────────
- To identify at least **three** reasons why the subject of war and warfare is so often taught in schools, colleges and universities.

War and warfare have played a very significant part in world history. Many of the world's key individuals, events, developments, inventions and changes are linked in some way to war and warfare. It is a brutal, controversial and very relevant topic that raises fascinating moral questions. In fact, it's everything a good history topic should be! So what makes the study of war and warfare so important? And what, exactly, is the difference between them?

War is relevant today and will be in the future

It is very rare that a week (or even a day) goes by without a report, feature or article in a newspaper, TV programme or online about war. It might be about the impact of war, or the cost of war, or a report on a **battle** or attack. It might focus on British troops somewhere in the world, or on other nations at war in distant lands. In the last few years alone there have been major wars in Iraq, Afghanistan and in several African nations. Britain has played a major part in the wars in Iraq and Afghanistan and these wars have had a significant impact on Britain too (as Sources A and B show). It is widely believed that Britain will continue to play a key role in other wars in years to come.

> **REVEALED: £12 billion hidden costs of Afghan War**
> The soaring cost of Britain's military campaign in Afghanistan is laid bare today, as a comprehensive analysis reveals that the cost of fighting the Taliban has passed £12 billion. An *Independent on Sunday* assessment of fighting since the Taliban was ousted in 2001 reveals that the bill works out at £190 for every man, woman and child in the UK – and would pay for 23 new hospitals, 60,000 new teachers or 77,000 new nurses.

⤺ **SOURCE B:** *From an article published in* The Independent *online newspaper, Sunday 26 July 2009, by Brian Brady and Jonathan Owen. The 'hidden costs' referred to money that will need to be spent in the future on support for injured troops and the families of those killed in action.*

⤺ **SOURCE A:** *War in today's world. Here, friends and family follow the coffin of a British soldier killed in Afghanistan as it leaves Coventry Cathedral in September 2009. In June 2010, it was announced that the number of UK service personnel killed in the Afghanistan War since 2001 had reached 300.*

War has had a huge impact on Britain and the world

The impact of war and warfare on Britain and the world has been enormous. Throughout history, wars have helped create great empires… and have also led to their demise. Wars have resulted in great cities being turned to rubble and vast areas of fertile farmland being churned into useless mud. Wars can create national heroes and infamous villains and can bring about major advances, in technology, medicine and the role of women, for example. But war is also one of the most destructive forces on the planet. In the twentieth century alone, it has been estimated that between 160 and 240 million people died fighting in wars.

Before World War One, Britain was arguably the most powerful and richest country on Earth, with the largest empire the world has ever seen. By the time World War Two was over, the USA and Soviet Russia dominated world power, while Britain was massively in debt – a debt that was only paid off in 2006! Source C outlines some other effects that the largest war in history had on the world.

'World War Two saw the introduction of radar and electronic warfare, sonar, hand-held antitank weapons. The jet engine, the cruise missile, and the smart bomb. The war also saw the first widespread use of antibiotics, blood plasma, synthetic insecticides and two-way radios in warfare. And finally, World War Two saw the creation of the V2 rocket, the first vehicle capable of reaching outer space and when coupled with nuclear weapons, the first weapons system likely to destroy the human race.'

↰ SOURCE C: *From a World War Two website, www.timemoneyandblood.com.*

WISE-UP Words

battle

war

warfare

The topic of war and warfare promotes debate

In February 2003, around 1 million people marched through London protesting about Britain's involvement in the Iraq War. It was the country's biggest ever demonstration and was one of many 'anti-war protests' that have taken place over the years against lots of different wars. Indeed, whenever any country goes to war, it always sparks fierce debate within that country in newspapers, on TV and in radio programmes. It is therefore very important that young people know as much as they can about war and warfare so that they can form their own opinion on such an important topic.

↰ SOURCE D: *Protest marchers outside the White House in Washington in November 1965. They are protesting about American involvement in the Vietnam War.*

War and warfare are fascinating topics

Let's not forget one of the best reasons to study wars and warfare – because it's usually a thoroughly absorbing story of politics, greed, bravery, tragedy, adventure, invention, honour, sacrifice and lots more (see Source E)!

↵ SOURCE E: *The amazing Douglas Bader, pictured on the wing of a Hurricane fighter plane – he is someone who makes the study of war truly fascinating! Born in London in 1910, Bader lost both his legs in a flying accident in 1931. However, he recovered, learned how to walk with artificial legs, retrained as a fighter pilot and joined the Royal Air Force. During World War Two he became a 'fighter ace' and fought in the Battle of Britain. In 1941 he was shot down over France and sent to a prisoner of war (POW) camp... without one of his artificial legs (it had remained trapped in his plane). However, the Germans allowed a British plane to drop off a new leg for him, and he managed to escape! When he was recaptured, he tried to escape again... so the Germans threatened to take both his artificial legs away. Bader survived the war, was knighted for his services to disabled people in 1976, and died in 1982.*

War and warfare shaped Britain's landscape and national identity

Nearly all towns in Britain have a war memorial of some kind – they are usually in town parks, community areas or on the main high street (see Source F). In some cities and towns, the damage from German bombing during World War Two was so severe that whole areas of housing, factories and public buildings had to be rebuilt after the war. Many of these places still stand today (see Sources G and H).

↖ **SOURCE F:** *A World War One Memorial in the small town of Lye, near Stourbridge, West Midlands. The statue also commemorates the local soldiers who were killed in World War Two.*

↵ **SOURCE G:** *A photograph of a burnt-out Coventry Cathedral, November 1940. It was bombed during the 'Coventry Blitz' of World War Two.*

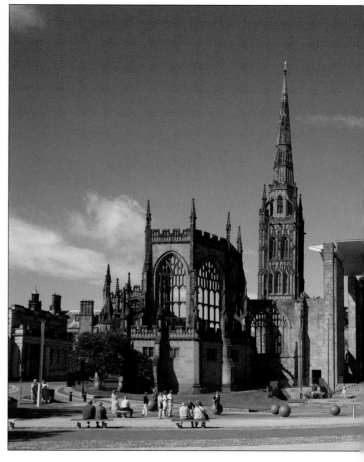

✚ Hungry for **MORE**

There will be buildings, monuments, places, streets and parks near you that are named after wars and battles or well-known people connected with them. For instance, London is full of them – Nelson's Column, Waterloo Station (and Waterloo Bridge) and Trafalgar Square are some well-known examples. There will almost certainly be a pub near you called the Lord Nelson, The Saracen's Head or the Trafalgar. Find out about places in Britain (perhaps near to *your* home) that are connected to, named after or linked in some way to wars and warfare.

SOURCE I: *In 2002 the BBC conducted a nationwide survey about 'Great Britons'. The result was a 'Top 100 Greatest Britons' and the person who came top and earned the title 'Greatest Briton' was wartime leader Winston Churchill. In fact, in the 'Top 100', around 20% were linked in some way to war and warfare!* ↱

SOURCE H: *Coventry Cathedral today. The old 'blitzed' Cathedral is on the left, whilst the new, modern one was built right next to it and opened in 1962.* ↴

War and warfare have become part of British life. Even today, people still refer to how two World Wars 'pulled the nation together', despite all the hardships they brought. Many Brits still take great pride in famous British victories from the pages of history – against the Spanish Armada and at Agincourt, Trafalgar and Waterloo, for example. People associated with wars, such as Francis Drake, Horatio Nelson, the Duke of Wellington, Florence Nightingale and Winston Churchill, have become instantly recognisable as national heroes and are remembered through street names, pub signs and monuments all over Britain (see Source I).

FACT So what's the difference?

The difference between war and warfare is simple. A 'war' is the name given to the act of fighting between two or more groups, nations or countries, whilst 'warfare' is the tactics, methods, strategies and science involved in fighting the enemy. So, for example, chemical warfare (a tactic to help you win) was used in The Great War (the name of the conflict).

FACT So what's a battle?

A battle is a fight (lasting days, weeks or months) between two opposing armies in a particular place. The Battle of Hastings in 1066, for example, lasted one day, whilst the Battle of Britain was fought between July and October 1940. Battles are usually part of a war... and wars often consist of many different battles.

Work

1 Imagine you've told someone at home (a parent, carer, brother or sister, for example) that you've just started the topic of 'War and Warfare' at school. In response, they ask you 'Why are you studying that?'

In full sentences, write down what you'd say in response to their question. Use the information on pages 6 to 9 to help you structure your answers.

2 What is the difference between:
i) war and warfare?
ii) wars and battles?

3 a Make a list of all the i) battles and ii) wars that you've studied at school before, or learned about independently.
b Did you enjoy studying them? If so, which ones, and why? If not, can you think of reasons?

MISSION ACCOMPLISHED?

• In your opinion, do you think it is appropriate that young people are taught about wars and warfare?

What is a war?

Before starting to look through the information on these pages, work with a partner or small group to 'brainstorm' all the words and phrases that you think of when you hear the word 'war'. Look after your work carefully – you'll need it later when you are asked to write your own definition of the word 'war'.

Defining war

There are many different definitions of 'war'. Generally speaking, though, they define war in a similar way, summed up as follows:

- War is a violent conflict between two or more countries, states or groups.

- War usually involves a long series of battles using the latest weapons.

- There are many different reasons why wars break out.

- Wars are usually fought by specially trained people (such as soldiers, sailors or airmen), but ordinary people (civilians) can become involved too.

- Wars can result in a huge number of deaths – over 70 million people (military and civilian) died in World War Two.

Why do wars start?

Wars break out for all sorts of reasons. Sometimes one single factor can lead to war, but more often than not it is a combination of different reasons. Source A tries to summarize some of the many, many reasons why wars start.

RESOURCES:

Countries have gone to war over resources time and time again. Throughout history nations have attacked others to gain natural resources like oil, coal, iron ore, gold and diamonds. In 1931, Japan attacked China for this reason.

LAND:

Wars have been fought because one country wanted another country's land, either as living space or to gain important features like islands or ports. Many nations have fought over the island of Malta, for example, because its location in the Mediterranean Sea is seen as an important strategic position.

TRADE:

Sometimes countries have fought over control of the seas and the trade routes between different places. The English and the Dutch fought a series of trade wars in the 17th and 18th centuries.

RELIGION:

Many wars have been fought for religious reasons. Between 1095 and 1291, for example, a series of religious 'Crusades' took place to try to restore Christian control of the Holy Land around Jerusalem. These 'Wars of the Cross' were fought mainly between European Christians and Muslims who had occupied the Holy Land for hundreds of years.

↰ SOURCE A: *The different reasons why wars start.*

'It's a fatal error to leave out the human element when thinking about wars. It is human beings who invented war, run it, wage it. Every decision in war, from entering it to sorting the mess out afterwards, is made by individual human beings, sometimes on their own, sometimes by default. Those who influence them have a choice too. The use of war is never compulsory, whatever reasons people may come up with to persuade you that it is.'

⤵ **SOURCE B:** *From the anti-war website set up by the Peace Pledge Union (www.ppu.org.uk).*

WISE-UP Words

civil war

'War is merely the continuation of politics by other means.'

⤵ **SOURCE C:** *A famous quote about war by Carl Von Clausewitz, a German soldier and writer (1780–1831).*

INDEPENDENCE:

Lots of wars have been fought by people who wish to gain their freedom (or independence) from a country or group that controls them. The American War of Independence (1775–1783) is a good example of this. Sometimes groups within the same country fight each other over various issues. This is called **civil war**.

PERSONAL GLORY:

Throughout history, leaders have attacked other nations and groups to achieve status and personal glory. In Tudor times, Henry VIII of England and Francis I of France both shared a taste for going to war with each other! To them, war was a way of gaining personal glory and international reputation. This was one of the reasons Italy's leader (Mussolini) attacked Ethiopia in 1935.

REASONS FOR WAR

REVENGE:

Sometimes the leader of one nation attacks another to get revenge. They wish to take back what they think is rightfully theirs, or put right something that they believe is wrong. For example, Alexander the Great (356–323 BCE) attacked the armies of the Persian Empire to revenge the Persian invasion of Greece.

MORAL REASONS:

Countries will sometimes attack others to defend the weak from violence. In 2011, the UK (with many other countries) launched missile attacks against Libya to try and stop Libyan leader Colonel Gaddafi attacking his own people.

! FACT Complex Causes

Wars very rarely start for just one reason. Usually the underlying causes go back a long way (long-term causes) and then the conflict begins when one or two smaller things 'spark it off' (short-term causes). World War Two is a classic example of this – the reason why the biggest conflict in human history began, and why so many different countries got involved, is a combination of all sorts of different factors.

What are the different types of war?

There have been many hundreds of wars – and in recent years experts have tried to put them into categories. Some wars fit neatly into a single category, whilst others can fit into several. These pages outline some of the main types of war fought throughout history.

Civil wars: Wars between different groups within the same country. For example, between 1642 and 1649, the English Civil War was fought between people who supported the king (Cavaliers) and those who supported Parliament (Roundheads).

SOURCE D: *Cavalier Prince Rupert charging at Edgehill, the first battle of English Civil War.* ↱

Revolutionary wars: When a large group within a country rises up in revolution against the rulers of the nation. Their aim is to gain their independence by replacing the current government. The American Revolutionary War is a good example. Sometimes these wars are known as 'wars of independence'. Indeed, the American Revolutionary War is also known as the American War of Independence.

Wars of religion: When people of one religion fight against people of another religion, or even a different group from the same religion who have slightly different beliefs or ways of worshipping. Between 1524 and 1648 a number of religious wars took place all over Europe – in Switzerland, France, Germany, Austria, England, Scotland, Ireland, the Netherlands and Denmark, for example.

↵ **SOURCE E:** *The Siege of Antioch in Turkey during the First Crusade in 1098. 'Crusade' was the name given to wars between European Christians and Middle Eastern Muslims between 1095 and 1291.*

World wars: There have been two of these. From 1914 to 1918 and from 1939 to 1945, countries from all over the world (formed into two huge alliances) fought against each other.

Nuclear wars: Wars in which nuclear weapons are the main weapon. Although nuclear weapons have been used in warfare (at the end of World War Two), they weren't the main weapons used in the conflict, and thankfully they haven't been used again since. Nuclear warfare is an example of a type of warfare that is named after the main weapon used – chemical warfare is another.

✚ Hungry for **MORE**

The landscape and environment in which a war takes place has a big impact on the fighting. Soldiers have to be trained to fight in particular conditions. Why not find some examples of soldiers fighting in the following environments:

- Arctic warfare
- Jungle warfare
- Sub-aquatic warfare
- Urban warfare
- Desert warfare
- Naval warfare
- Alpine warfare
- Electronic warfare

Guerilla wars: When a small group within a country stages raids and ambushes on larger groups of government soldiers or enemy forces who occupy land that the guerillas believe belongs to them. 'Guerilla' is a Spanish term for 'little war', and guerilla soldiers (in little teams) hide and fight in forests and mountains. During the Vietnam War (1955–1975), Vietcong guerilla units inflicted huge losses on US troops fighting there.

↵ SOURCE F:
A Vietnamese soldier coming out of a tunnel. During the Vietnam War, guerrilla soldiers used tunnels to sneak up on and surprise the enemy.

Work

1 a In your own words, define 'war'.
  b Was it easy to write a definition of war of not? Explain your answer.
2 a Explain how each of the following can lead to or cause war:
    i resources
    ii land
    iii trade
    iv religion
    v independence
    vi revenge
    vii personal glory
    viii moral reasons
  b Can you think of any other reasons why countries go to war?
  c Try to remember three different wars you've studied, perhaps in school History classes, and next to each one, explain which of the reasons listed caused it. Remember that there may be a combination of causes.
3 Look at Source B.
  a What points are being made by the author?
  b Do you agree with what is being said?
4 Design a poster, diagram or leaflet that explains the different types of warfare. Make it simple, colourful and don't use huge paragraphs of writing in your explanations!
5 What is the difference between 'conventional' and 'unconventional' warfare?

Proxy wars: Wars in which major countries do not actually fight each other, for various reasons. Instead they get involved in smaller wars and take opposite sides. A good example is the Korean War (1950–1953) in which South Korea (supported by the USA) fought against North Korea (supported mainly by China but also the Soviet Union).

Terrorism: The use of terrorist acts (bombings, assassinations, hijackings etc.) to make political points. Many people now recognize terrorism as a type of war. Most terror groups are well organized and choose targets like airports, trains and public buildings to achieve maximum media coverage.

Total war: Where the entire country works together to beat the enemy, from soldiers in the front lines to women back home in the factories making the weapons, battleships and tanks. The whole country also becomes a target, because any form of attack is to be expected. In World War One, for example, German bomber planes and air balloons bombed towns and cities from the air, killing over 1,000 people.

! FACT Conventional versus Unconventional

Conventional warfare is the use of armies, navies and air forces to fight enemy forces on battlefields, in the air and at sea. The aim is to wear down and beat your enemy into surrender. This is sometimes called 'attritional warfare' – 'attrition' means 'to wear away'. This is how most wars throughout history have been fought. Unconventional warfare is the use of creative, innovative and even bizarre methods and tactics to attack your enemy. The idea is to surprise, harass and terrorize the enemy, and civilians can become targets too. Unconventional warfare is often carried out by small groups who make small strikes time and time again, hoping to force their enemy to give up.

—— MISSION ACCOMPLISHED? ——

• Are you able to explain five reasons why wars start, list five different types of war and describe five different environments in which warfare takes place?

Who does the fighting in a war?

———————————— MISSION OBJECTIVES ————————————

- To understand (and be able to explain in your own words) what is meant by the term 'armed forces'… and to identify its three key elements.

Look at Source A and think about what you can see. You may have noted that the painting shows three of the key elements involved in fighting a war – the army, navy and air force. This painting, set during World War Two, shows soldiers from the British Army desperately trying to get out to British ships that have come to rescue them from the beaches of Dunkirk, France in 1940. German bombers and fighter planes are trying to stop the rescue. So are soldiers in the army, sailors in the navy and pilots in the air force the only people who fight wars? How do governments get people to fight in the first place? And how do ordinary civilians contribute to wars?

⤆ SOURCE A: *A painting showing the British retreat from the beaches of Dunkirk, 1940.*

The Armed Forces

Wars are mainly fought by specially trained people known collectively as the armed forces, and this usually includes the army, navy and air force. Most countries have armed forces and their specific role is to defend the country if attacked, and to attack others if ordered to do so by the country's leaders.

FACT Women at War
Many countries allow women to join their armed forces. Since the early 1990s, women have been allowed to join Britain's armed forces – but are prevented from being involved in close combat where they may be required to fight hand-to-hand with an enemy.

FACT Do I have to join?
The British Armed Forces are voluntary, but in times of warfare (such as the Great War and World War Two) Britain has introduced **conscription**. This was when the government passed a law that said all men (between 18 and 41) could be 'called up' to fight if required.

The Army

What?

An army is a group of people recruited and trained by a country to protect that country and fight its enemies. Currently the largest army in the world is China's with over 2 million people!

Who?

Anyone who serves in the army is called a soldier. They fight on land and are specially trained to use a variety of weapons and fill a range of roles. Specific roles include:

- **Tankers** – soldiers trained as part of a tank crew.

- **Sappers/Engineers** – soldiers who build bridges, repair airfields, clear minefields…and fight.

- **Snipers** – marksmen able to shoot accurately at targets from a great distance with a specialist rifle.

- **Infantryman** – fit, strong, disciplined soldiers who fight on foot. In warfare, casualties are usually highest amongst this group of soldiers.

- **Paratroopers** – soldiers trained to parachute onto enemy positions from helicopters or aircraft.

There are currently 110,000 soldiers in the British Army, which is the second largest in the European Union. In World War Two, by contrast, over 3.5 million men served in Britain's army… and nearly 400,000 died.

⤴ **SOURCE B:** *The first picture shows soldiers in action in the 18th century, and the second shows British soldiers in Afghanistan in 2010. Can you see any differences and similarities between soldiers past and present?*

Air force

What?

A country's air force is the part of their armed forces that uses aircraft. In some places it is known as an air army. The main job of an air force during a war is to gain control of the air, carry out bombing missions and provide support to soldiers fighting on the ground below.

Who?

A person who flies a fighter plane, bomber, transport plane or helicopter is called a pilot, but there are many other jobs in an air force. These include weapons operators, analysts, air traffic controllers, technicians, drivers and medics.

Britain's air force, known as the Royal Air Force or RAF, is one of the oldest in the world. It was set up in 1918 and has played a significant role in Britain's wars ever since. The RAF currently has around 1000 aircraft and employs about 45,000 people. The largest air forces in the world belong to the USA, Russia and China. If a country has nuclear weapons, its air force is generally responsible for them.

↩ **SOURCE C:** *The World War I Sopwith Camel plane (left) and the modern RAF Jaguar jet (right).* ↱

The navy

What?

A navy is the part of a country's armed forces that fights on (or under) the sea. The term is used for surface warships and submarines, together with all the sailors, bases and supplies.

Who?

A person who serves in the navy is called a sailor or **seaman**. Like soldiers, they are specially trained for all types of jobs – weapons operators, communication specialists, mine clearance divers, aircraft carrier crew, chefs, nurses, radar operators, and many more. The navy also has its own version of soldiers who use helicopters, hovercraft and small boats to leave their warships and attack the enemy. These are called **marines**.

Britain's Royal Navy is one of the oldest in the world, created in the 1500s by King Henry VIII. For most of its history it was the world's largest navy – at one point during World War Two it had 900 warships! Today's Royal Navy is much smaller, with about 90 warships including submarines, destroyers and mine-sweepers. Around 30,000 people currently serve in the Royal Navy – a sharp contrast to the US Navy, which has over 300,000 sailors and nearly 300 ships and submarines. The US Navy is the world's largest. Even if the 12 next biggest navies in the world all joined together... it would still be bigger!

↵ SOURCE D: *Royal Navy – past and present. The first picture shows a scene from the Spanish Armada of 1588, when Spain's navy (the Armada) tried to invade England. The ship on the right is named* Ark Royal. *In the second picture a modern Royal Navy ship is shown. Interestingly, this is also called* Ark Royal. ↴

It isn't just the army, navy and air force that contribute when a country is at war. Ordinary civilians, resistance fighters and even animals have all made their mark in warfare.

Resistance from within

Sometimes people living in a country that has been invaded organize themselves into secret **resistance groups** to fight the enemy. They commit acts of **sabotage** like destroying bridges, dams and railway lines to disrupt and frustrate the occupiers.

Work ⌐‿⌐.

1 Look at Source A. The painting shows the three key elements that make up 'armed forces' – the army, navy and air force. In your own words, explain what is meant by an army, a navy and an air force.

2 Look at the pictures in the fact boxes on pages 15 and 16 and use what you see to make a list of similarities and differences between fighting in the past and fighting today in:
   • The army (Source B)
   • The air force (Source C)
   • The navy (Source D)

Total war

A **total war** is a war that involves both the armed forces and ordinary civilians. In other words, all groups in society, including women and children, become part of the war. This might mean:

- Civilians are targeted by enemy forces directly, either by bombing or by occupation of their country (see Source E).
- Ordinary people help defend the country by building coastal defences, clearing unexploded bombs, directing searchlights or operating anti-aircraft guns.

⭐ **WISE-UP** Words

conscription

marines

resistance group

sabotage

total war

SOURCE E: *This Surrey home was bombed in a German air raid during World War Two. This bombing of Britain by the Nazis was known as 'The Blitz' and over 40,000 people were killed in raids over London, Birmingham, Manchester, Coventry, Bristol, Cardiff, Glasgow and many more British cities.* ↱

SOURCE F: *Female workers during World War One, contributing to the war effort by making bombs and bullets. Women took over many of the jobs traditionally done by men during the war, becoming bus drivers, police officers and car mechanics. They worked on farms, or as nurses or ambulance drivers near the front lines.* ↳

FOOD FOR THE GUNS.

Work

1 a Write a summary of what is meant by the term 'armed forces'.
  b What qualities do you think are required to be a soldier in today's army?

2 Who else, apart from people in the armed forces, contribute in some way during war?

3 a What is the difference between a 'serviceman' and a 'civilian'?
  b What do you understand by the term 'total war'?

✚ Hungry for MORE

For thousands of years, animals have contributed to warfare... even by fighting! Find out when, where and how some of the following animals have played their part:
- Dogs • Elephants • Rats • Pigeons • Horses

---MISSION ACCOMPLISHED?---

- Can you explain what is meant by the term 'armed forces'?
- Can you describe at least three ways in which individuals or groups other than members of the armed forces fight or contribute during wartime?

WEAPONS OF WAR

A **weapon** is an item designed or used to harm or kill a person, or to damage (or destroy) property. They help you gain an advantage over your enemy on land, on sea, in the air… or even in outer space! They can also be used to defend against attack. Weapons can be used by individuals or large groups (such as an army of soldiers). They can be improvised (like a rock found lying around and thrown) or they can be specially built, hi-tech machines that can cause huge damage and loss of life (for example, laser-guided missiles). This Depth Study will take you on a journey through the development of **weaponry** (as the invention and production of weapons is known) through the ages – from the prehistoric beginnings of weapons such as spears and clubs to the nuclear age and beyond.

1: Weapons of the ancient world

MISSION OBJECTIVES

- To understand how the discovery of metal-making changed weaponry.
- To know the key differences between hand-held weapons and larger 'war machines'.

What were the earliest weapons like?

The oldest weapons ever discovered were a group of eight wooden spears. They were found in a mine in Germany in 1998 and experts think they are about 400,000 years old. Prehistoric humans (often known as 'cavemen') used all sorts of basic weapons, including wooden clubs, axes (made from sharp stone and wood), slings and throwing sticks (like boomerangs). The oldest **atl-atl** dates back nearly 30,000 years. This was an instrument used to help a person throw their spear even further. A common dog-ball thrower (made from plastic and used for hurling a tennis ball) is a modern version of an atl-atl.

⤴ SOURCE A: *A cave painting found in Algeria showing a prehistoric hunting scene. You can make out the shapes of weapons that would have been used.*

How did metal change things?

Wooden and stone weapons have their limitations. For a start, they break quite easily and it is hard to get them very sharp. But when people began to work metal (around 5000 years ago), weapon-making changed forever. Metals like copper, bronze (which is copper and tin mixed together) and iron meant that swords and daggers could be made. These weapons are tough, sharp and can slice things easily. Soon metal tips were being fitted to the ends of spears, lances and arrows, making them even deadlier.

What about bigger weapons?

Weapons of the ancient world weren't just small, hand-held items like swords, spears, axes and maces. Larger weapons or 'war machines' were also used to attack an enemy. Horse-drawn **chariots**, for example, were used all over the ancient world – in China, Egypt, Persia, Rome and Britain (see Source B). Special machines like **battering rams** and **catapults** were also used to fight an enemy. These war machines might be designed to kill or harm enemy soldiers or batter down the walls of enemy forts or cities (see Source C).

Sometimes an army would not use war chariots like the one in Source B. Instead, the soldiers would just ride on the horses and charge at their enemy with swords and spears. Soldiers specializing in fighting on horseback are called **cavalry**. They are said to be the third oldest type of soldier – after infantry (foot soldiers) and charioteers (soldiers in chariots).

WISE-UP Words

atl-atl   battering ram
catapult   cavalry   chariot
weapon   weaponry

⌐ **SOURCE B:** *A war chariot from the ancient world. Note the blades on the wheels and the spears fitted to the front of the horses.*

⌐ **SOURCE C:** *A catapult, which was used to fire massive arrows at enemy soldiers. A battering ram was a huge log that was swung at an enemy wall to knock it down.*

War and warriors

War played an important role in the ancient world. Some tribes or groups fought to protect themselves while others fought to conquer land and build empires. The Romans, for example, first fought against their neighbours to protect their own city (Rome). As time went by, they fought further and further from Rome and took huge amounts of new territory. At its largest, the Roman Empire stretched for 2500 miles, from northern Britain across Europe to Egypt in northern Africa. In fact, the Roman soldier is probably one of the best examples of a warrior of the ancient world (see Source D).

SOURCE D: *War in the ancient world was brutal. It was a bit like a mass brawl with everyone piling in. Sometimes one side would panic and run away... but the Romans hardly ever did this. They were renowned for their organization, bravery and brilliant military tactics and weaponry.* ↱

Work

1 What's the difference between a spear and an atl-atl?

2 **a** In what ways did the discovery of metal-making change weaponry?
  b Can you think of any other examples of how new technology has changed weaponry?

3 **a** Explain what you think the difference is between a 'personal weapon' and a 'war machine'.
  b In your own words, describe how the following weapons are used:
   • chariot   • battering ram
   • catapult

4 In what ways did the Roman Army help to build the Roman Empire?

___ **MISSION ACCOMPLISHED?** ___

Can you list **three** characteristics common to weapons of the ancient world?

The period known as the Middle Ages (from around 1066 up to the arrival of the Tudors in 1485) was extremely violent. There were fierce struggles between different groups *within* countries – and vicious clashes as some nations invaded others. It was the time of castles and knights… and some of the most brutal weapons ever designed. So just how deadly were these weapons?

2: Which weapons would *you* use?

MISSION OBJECTIVES

- To remember what at least five different weapons from the Middle Ages looked like and how they worked.
- To say how effective you think each of these weapons might have been on the battlefield.

Who did the fighting?

There were two basic types of fighting man in the Middle Ages. First there were the **knights**, who were highly-trained warriors of 'noble birth' who swore to be faithful to their king, country and religion. These knights were given land by the king in return for loyalty and help when the king required it. There were also ordinary foot soldiers called **infantry**, who worked on the knight's land for most of the year and fought for him when the king asked the knight for help.

A Knight's horse: *These were big and chunky so they could carry the weight of a knight in full armour.*

B Armour: *The first armour was made out of thick leather. Later it was made from tough pieces of metal fixed together with joints.*

C Lance: *A long spear tipped with iron or steel.*

D Arrows: *A skilled archer could fire 10–12 of the three-foot-long arrows per minute. They were tipped with steel, with some arrows designed to pierce armour whilst others could bring down a knight's horse!*

E English longbow: *One of the deadliest weapons on the battlefield, it could be fired from over 200 metres away. Around six feet long and made from wood with a linen string. Several English kings introduced laws that made it compulsory for men to practise their archery skills in their spare time! At the Battle of Crecy in 1346, nearly 2000 French knights and soldiers were killed by English longbow men. The English lost just 50 men!*

F Crossbow: *Mini wooden catapults used to fire bolts through armour at a range of over 100 metres. Easier to use than a longbow but it couldn't fire as far.*

G Chainmail shirt: *Some of the wealthier foot soldiers and knights wore long shirts made from small metal rings linked together to form a mesh.*

H Battleaxe: *Razor-sharp axe that could slice off an arm or leg in a single blow.*

I Pike: *A long wooden pole tipped with steel. Knights on horseback could be brought to the ground by stabbing the horse beneath them.*

J Mace: *A heavy, metal club with sharp edges. They could shatter bones and crush skulls.*

K Caltrop: *Iron spike thrown on the ground in order to stab through the feet of charging horses and men.*

L Flail: *A heavy metal spiked ball on a chain. Often used to stick into armour and drag knights off their horses.*

M Helmet: *To protect the head and neck.*

N Shield: *For protection from heavy blows and decorated with a coat of arms.*

O Bombard: *An early type of cannon from around 1400. Gunpowder was loaded into one end and blown up, and a heavy stone or metal ball flew out of the other end.*

P Swords and daggers: *Swords were large chopping weapons whilst daggers were carried in case a soldier lost their main weapon in the chaos of the battle and needed to carry on fighting in close contact.*

Siege warfare

The Middle Ages is known for its sieges. A siege was a situation where one group of soldiers were outside a castle or city trying to get in, whilst the people inside tried to keep them out. Sieges could last for weeks, months or even years! All sorts of weapons were used by both sides against each other. For example, attackers used battering rams, ladders and huge catapults (called trebuchets) to try and get in, whilst the defenders dropped rocks or poured boiling water on the attackers and fired arrows at them to keep them out!

Work

1 Write a sentence or two to explain the following terms:
   i infantry
   ii siege

2 a Make two lists: one of weapons used to attack, and the other of weapons used for defence.
   b Do any weapons appear on both lists?

3 Either: Imagine you own a medieval weapons shop. Design a website homepage (on paper) that describes the weapons you sell, shows a picture and explains how effective each weapon is and how it's used.
   Or: Imagine a TV company has asked you to prepare a short programme on medieval weapons. Design a storyboard outlining the five weapons or items you would include.

—— MISSION ACCOMPLISHED? ——

• Could you explain the differences between a pike, a flail, a crossbow, a longbow and a bombard?

For many years, fighting in a war meant getting up close and personal. Unless you were an archer standing hundreds of metres away, fighting an enemy meant you'd be close enough to see the fear in their eyes and feel your weapon crunch through their bones and get covered in their blood! You had to stand toe-to-toe with your enemy, trading blows with them until one of you went down. If the enemy wasn't out on the battlefield but holed up in a walled town or castle instead, then battles could go on for months. Most towns and castles were so well built, with thick, well-defended walls, that catapults throwing stones and battering rams smashing into walls took a long time to make any impact. But one invention changed all this… gunpowder!

3: Boom!

MISSION OBJECTIVES

- To assess the importance of the invention of gunpowder in warfare.

The invention of gunpowder

Gunpowder was first used in China around 2000 years ago. It was discovered by accident by Chinese scholars searching for a potion to give eternal life. Gunpowder (or 'Fire Medicine' as the Chinese called it) is a mixture of three ingredients – sulphur (a chemical mined out of the ground), charcoal (a form of half-burnt wood) and potassium nitrate (a chemical made from old animal dung and urine). If these are mixed together in the right quantities then a highly explosive substance is formed, known as gunpowder.

The Chinese first used gunpowder to make loud 'fire flowers' to frighten off evil spirits (these are still around today, but we know them as 'fireworks'). Then, around 1000 years ago, Chinese investors realized that you could also use gunpowder to make weapons. Chinese soldiers put small stone balls and rocks inside bamboo tubes and shot them out by lighting gunpowder at one end. Basically, this is the same idea that makes guns and rifles work today!

Chinese fireworks

For years Chinese emperors managed to keep their deadly discovery secret, but eventually other people also found out how to use gunpowder to make weapons. By the 1300s, inventors in China, the Middle East and Europe had come up with what became known as cannons (from the Latin *canna*, meaning 'large tube'). Initially called **bombards**, these early cannons were used to hurl heavy iron balls (called cannonballs) at the walls of castles or towns under

⤷ SOURCE A: *A picture from 1390 showing European knights using cannons against an African city.*

attack. Before long, castles and town walls became useless because a group of well-aimed cannons could fire their cannonballs through anything (see Source A). By the late 1400s, cannons could fire heavy stone or iron balls over a mile. It didn't take long before cannons were put on ships too… and the battleship was born!

The birth of the handgun

As well as large cannons, people in the 1300s also began to use smaller, hand-held versions called 'hand cannons'. Soon these developed into **muskets**, an early type of **rifle**, and then into even smaller versions called **handguns** (see Source B).

Over the next few hundred years, musketeers (soldiers who used muskets) and riflemen replaced archers and crossbowmen. Musket-balls and bullets fired from these new weapons reached such high speeds that soon they could pierce even the very best armour. In fact, guns (a collective word for rifles, muskets, handguns, etc.) soon became the main weapon that ordinary soldiers took into battle. The widespread use of gunpowder to fire bullets and balls across battlefields marked the end of the age of the lance, shield and sword as the world's most decisive weapons (see Source C).

SOURCE B: *The development of the handgun.*

Early hand cannon (1300s) – *the user lights the gunpowder in a small tube, which fires a small ball (or bullet) out of the end.* ▼

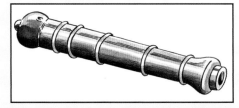

Matchlock musket (1400s) – *the first mechanically firing gun.* ▼

Wheel lock guns (1509) – *a wheel spins and generates a spark that ignites the gunpowder to fire the musket-ball from the chamber.* ▼

Flintlock guns (1630s) – *a flint (stone) strikes a* frizzen *(an L-shaped piece of metal) to make a spark. The spark ignites the gunpowder.* ▼

Percussion cap guns (1825) – *a metal hammer strikes a small metal cylinder with a tiny amount of explosive material inside. This replaced the need for the spark in earlier guns.* ▼

Colt revolver (1835) – *the first mass-produced, multi-shot, revolving chamber handgun.* ▼

Shotgun (1850) – *the explosive primer material and pellets are all contained in a tube (or 'shell') together. On firing, a compacted mass of pellets (the 'shot') blasts through anything in its way.* ▼

Gatling gun (1862) – *a gun with numerous barrels that were rotated by a user with a hand crank. This allowed very rapid firing of each barrel in turn.* ▼

Magazine-fed Lee Enfield rifle (1895) – *bullets are loaded into the rifle via a spring-activated magazine, allowing up to 10 bullets to be fired as quickly as one every 2 seconds.* ▼

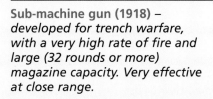

Sub-machine gun (1918) – *developed for trench warfare, with a very high rate of fire and large (32 rounds or more) magazine capacity. Very effective at close range.*

▶

AK47 (1947) – *the first assault rifle, developed for use in close-quarters fighting where rate of fire and ease of use were more important. Cheap to make, reliable and simple to use, it has been used worldwide for 60 years.*

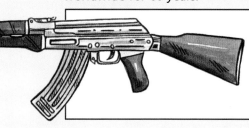

'In the fifteenth century, however, gunpowder and firearms began to come into general use, and no castle could stand up against a bombardment... The local lord could no longer retreat into his fortress for safety, and when it came to fighting out in the open, his strong, expensive armour, which was proof against a foot soldier's arrows, was no protection against a bullet from the clumsiest gun fired by the humblest peasant.'

↳ SOURCE C: *From a modern school textbook,* History Alive 1, *by Peter Moss (Hart-Davis Educational, 1980).*

WISE-UP Words

bombard
frizzen   handgun
musket   rifle

Work

1 Write down five facts about gunpowder.

2 In your own words, write a definition of a:
   i bombard   ii musket   iii handgun

3 Each of the following dates is important in the history of the handgun:
   1825; 1918; 1947; 1509; 1630s; 1862; 1300s; 1835; 1850; 1400s; 1895
   Write them out in the correct chronological order, and then explain why they are important in gun history.

4 Look at Source C. According to this source, how did the invention of gunpowder and firearms change warfare?

—— MISSION ACCOMPLISHED? ——

• Are you able to judge for yourself, and then explain to a friend, how important the invention of gunpowder was in warfare?

Before the arrival of gunpowder on the battlefield, weapons were mainly human-powered. A sword could only hit someone as hard as the soldier could swing it, and a spear could only travel as far as the warrior could throw it. There were other types of weapon too, like battering rams, catapults and longbows, but again these were either powered by humans or by springs and weights. Gunpowder changed all this. The energy released by exploding gunpowder could propel bullets, balls and stones over great distances at incredibly high speeds. Over time, better and more accurate gunpowder-powered weapons gradually replaced swords, lances and pikes as war's most effective weapons.

4: Deadly weapons of the modern world

―――――――――――――― MISSION OBJECTIVES ――――――――――――――
• To understand the origins of some of the modern world's most effective weapons.

A weapons revolution

During the 1800s there were enormous advances in technology and the use of machines. Engineers and skilled craftsmen could make all sorts of things better, quicker, stronger and more reliable than ever before. Such advances meant that weapons improved too. Rifles became more reliable, cannons fired further and handguns were more accurate. And there was a whole host of brand new weaponry, specially designed to create bloodshed and cause death on an unimaginable scale. Study the following Fact Files carefully so you can judge some of the modern world's most deadly weapons for yourself.

RIFLE

A rifle is a type of long gun that is held against the shoulder. A pattern of grooves (called '**rifling**') are cut into the barrel (the long tube where the bullets come out), which makes the bullets spin. This makes the bullet travel faster and straighter. Rifles have been around for over 200 years and have been continually improved during that time. They were the standard weapon given to all soldiers during World Wars One and Two.

ARTILLERY

Artillery is the name given to big guns and cannons that fire explosive shells over long distances. Artillery was used thousands of years ago – 'war machines' like catapults and trebuchets used a mechanical system to hurl rocks, stone balls and large arrows at enemy forces. However, the introduction of gunpowder in the Middle Ages meant that artillery could fire cannonballs much further. Over the next few hundred years, artillery weapons advanced rapidly and by the turn of the twentieth century there were guns that could fire shells over 75 miles.

TANKS

Tanks are armoured vehicles that can travel over rough ground, through hedgerows, over barbed wire and rubble, and even through walls! They can fire explosive shells and most have machine guns too. First used in World War One, tanks are considered one of the key weapons in a modern army. They rarely operate alone, but are organized into units of around 10–20 and go into battle supported by ground troops who accompany them on foot or in specially designed armoured trucks.

MACHINE GUN

Inventors tried for many years to make a gun that rapidly fired bullets in a continuous stream. In 1718 James Puckle came up with his 'Defence Gun', which could fire 63 bullets in seven minutes. By 1861 Richard Gatling had developed a gun that had six barrels and could fire over 300 shots in a minute. During World War One, all sides had machine guns that could fire up to 500 bullets a minute. They were heavy and needed a crew of five or six, but one machine gun was worth around 100 rifles. By World War Two, light machine guns had been developed that a single soldier could carry around. Today, some machine guns (weighing nearly 40kg) can fire around 4000 bullets per minute!

AEROPLANES

Aeroplanes were not invented until 1903, but by the start of World War One (1914) they were already being used in war. When fighting began they were used mainly for keeping an eye on the enemy. At first pilots fired pistols or threw bricks at enemy pilots, but soon 'fighter planes' armed with machine guns were developed. Not long after, 'bomber planes' were produced to fly over the enemy and drop bombs on them. By World War Two, a country's air force had become a key element of its armed forces. This is still the case today.

HAND GRENADE

A hand grenade is a small bomb that is thrown at an enemy and timed to explode a short time after release. They have been around for over 1000 years and were first used in the Middle East when soldiers packed ceramic jars with gunpowder and a slow-burning fuse. More modern hand grenades operate by removing a pin, which starts a timer set to explode after a short time. They were commonly used by all sides during the World Wars and are today part of any ordinary soldier's weaponry.

POISON GAS

Poisonous gas was used as a weapon as long ago as the 1600s, but it was during World War One that its use became common. The French first used tear gas at the beginning of the war, but soon most sides were using mustard gas (which burned the skin) and chlorine and phosgene gases (which attacked the lungs). In total, around 90,000 soldiers were killed by poison gas in World War One and 1.2 million were hospitalized. Today its use is banned by most of the world's major nations.

WARSHIPS

Warships have been used for thousands of years. The ancient Persians, Greeks and Romans used long wooden boats to ram and sink enemy ships or transport soldiers to battle. Cannons were added to warships in the 1500s and some countries, like Britain and Spain, used their warships to create huge empires around the world. Warships made from metal and powered by steam appeared in the 1800s and fighting at sea using warships has been a key element of warfare in the last few hundred years. Warships now have all sorts of different roles – to carry aircraft, or land troops on enemy beaches, or travel underwater (submarines) to fire missiles at enemy targets, for example.

WISE-UP Words

rifling

Work ‿‿‿.

1 In what ways did the invention of gunpowder change the way battles were fought?

2 Why, during the nineteenth century, did weapons become deadlier than ever?

3 **a** Draw this puzzle into your book and fill in the answers to the clues

1. Underwater warship
2. Used long wooden boats
3. Early inventor
4. Not a bomber plane
5. Big guns
6. Small hand bomb
7. Long gun
8. A type of poison gas
9. Another type
10. Tough, armoured vehicle

b Now read down the puzzle (clue 11) and write down five facts about this weapon.

c In your opinion, which is the modern world's deadliest weapon? Explain the reasons behind your choice.

—MISSION ACCOMPLISHED?—

• Could you write a sentence or two, in your own words, explaining the origins and use of **four** of the modern world's most deadly weapons?

Many countries fought in World War Two, but most of the fighting involved Britain, the USA and Russia against Germany, Italy and Japan. By May 1945, Germany and Italy had been defeated but Japan continued to fight. On Monday 6 August 1945, a US bomber plane dropped a single atomic bomb on the Japanese city of Hiroshima. 80,000 people were killed instantly, and 70,000 of the city's 78,000 buildings were flattened. Immediately people saw why the bomb's designer – the American Robert Oppenheimer – had called it 'the destroyer of worlds'. Three days later a second weapon was dropped on the port of Nagasaki with similar results. Japan surrendered on 10 August and World War Two officially ended. So what was the importance of this new weapon for the modern world?

5: 'The destroyer of worlds'

MISSION OBJECTIVES

• To be able to outline the features of some key weapons of the modern world.

↰ SOURCE A: *This is a photograph of a test explosion of a nuclear bomb on 25 July 1945. (You can see some of the old warships they used to test the blast.) The bomb dropped on Hiroshima was the equivalent of 20 000 tons of dynamite. When US President Truman heard of the bombing, he said, 'This is the greatest thing in history'.*

'Their faces were burned, their eye sockets hollow, the fluid from their melted eyes had run down their cheeks. Their mouths were mere swollen, pus-covered wounds, which they couldn't open wide enough to take a drink from a teapot.'

↰ SOURCE B: *A description of some men found hiding in bushes after the bombing (from J Hershey's account of the effects of the bomb, 1946, in SHP Peace and War by Shephard, Reid and Shephard, 1993).*

The rocket

World War Two saw major advances in weapons technology. Rifles and artillery became more accurate, machine guns were lighter and fired more bullets, and tanks and fighter planes became faster and more reliable. And there was a brand-new development: the Germans began using **rockets**. German scientists had been experimenting with rockets for years, and by World War Two they had developed rockets that could carry high explosives to targets hundreds of miles away (see Source C).

Space rockets

After the war, many of the German rocket scientists were captured and taken to work on rocket technology in the USA and Russia. By 1957, the Russians had developed rockets that could travel over 3500 miles (called InterContinental Ballistic Missiles or ICBMs), and could carry nuclear bombs. Rockets were also used to put satellites in space and in 1961, Russian Yuri Gagarin became the first human to journey into space… carried by a rocket! In 1969, the Americans used rockets to put man on the moon.

Rockets are still a common military weapon. The number of the largest rockets (ICBMs) has been greatly reduced, but smaller guided rockets or missiles are often used by ships, helicopters or fighter planes.

The Nuclear Age

The most powerful weapon invented in recent history is the nuclear bomb – but its power is actually one of the reasons why it hasn't been used in warfare since 1945. Any country using it to attack another would almost certainly face nuclear retaliation. This is known as **Mutually Assured Destruction** or MAD. By 1986, it was estimated that there were around 40,000 nuclear weapons throughout the world – the equivalent in power of one million Hiroshima bombs. This was more than enough to destroy every human on the planet! The effect of so much devastating power was a global fear of nuclear war and in the 1990s countries began to dismantle them. Today nuclear weapons still exist, but they are incredibly tightly controlled, and there are far fewer than in the 1980s.

➕ Hungry for **MORE**

What about the latest weapons… and the weapons of the future? Try to find out about EMPs (or E-bombs) and Directed Energy Weapons (DEWs), for example. Some countries have been trying to develop artificial black ice that can be sprayed on roads causing soldiers to fall over and vehicles to crash, and a high energy beam that radiates out over 500 metres and penetrates the skin to about 0.4 millimetres, causing a sensation that makes people think their clothes are on fire!

⭐ **WISE-UP** Words

Mutually Assured Destruction

rocket

↵ **SOURCE C:** *The German V2 long-range missile, the forerunner of modern space rockets, watched by German troops in 1944. It had a range of 200–220 miles, rose to a height of 50 miles and travelled at over 2000 mph. Over 3000 of these were launched at targets during World War Two, killing and injuring over 10,000 people.*

Work ⁓.

1 Why do you think the designer of the bombs dropped on Hiroshima and Nagasaki called it 'the destroyer of worlds'?

2 a What are rockets?
  b How can rockets be used in both positive and negative ways?
  c Can you think of any other examples where scientific breakthroughs and inventions have been used in both a positive and a negative way?
  d In what ways did German scientists help the Russian and the American space programmes?
  e Why do you think many people have criticised the Russians and Americans for doing this?
  f Russia put the first human in space whilst America put the first man on the moon – so who won the space race?

3 a What is MAD?
  b In what ways has MAD helped to prevent nuclear war?

—— **MISSION ACCOMPLISHED?** ——

• Can you differentiate between ICBMs, V2s, EMPs and DEWs?

How are wars and battles won?

_____ **MISSION OBJECTIVES** _____

• To ensure you can outline at least three different methods used to win battles and wars.

Look at Sources A and B. They show the methods and effects of a devastating military tactic used by the Germans with huge success during World War Two. It was called **blitzkrieg**, which means 'lightning war', and was used when defeating the Polish Army in 1939 and throughout Europe in 1940 and 1941. Put simply, the Germans concentrated all their military power to create a massive 'armoured fist' that could smash through enemy positions and cause chaos. It is an excellent example of one of the many methods, tactics and strategies used over the years by one army to beat another. So how else have wars and battles been won?

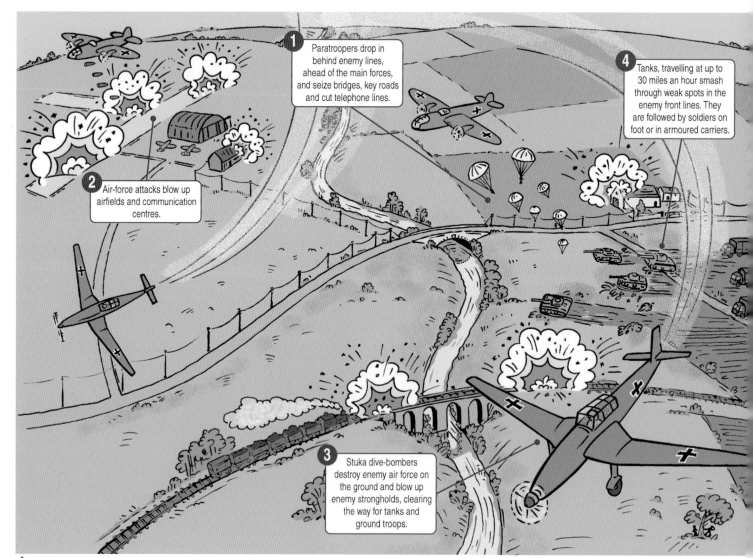

1. Paratroopers drop in behind enemy lines, ahead of the main forces, and seize bridges, key roads and cut telephone lines.

2. Air-force attacks blow up airfields and communication centres.

3. Stuka dive-bombers destroy enemy air force on the ground and blow up enemy strongholds, clearing the way for tanks and ground troops.

4. Tanks, travelling at up to 30 miles an hour smash through weak spots in the enemy front lines. They are followed by soldiers on foot or in armoured carriers.

↰ SOURCE A: _Based on speed, co-ordination and surprise, the idea with blitzkrieg was for tanks, supported by fighter planes, bomber planes and infantry (foot soldiers), to smash through enemy lines and create panic amongst ordinary civilians. As well as inflicting heavy losses as a result of the initial attack, the chaos caused by the invaders made it impossible for a defending army to get its forces to the war front, because ordinary people were fleeing in the opposite direction! It was designed to hit the enemy hard – and then allow attacking troops to move on quickly and hit the enemy again._

- 'When the dive-bombers come down, they [the French] stood it for two hours and then ran with their hands over their ears'.
- 'Sedan [a French town] fell as a result of a bombardment... it was a superb example of military surprise'.
- 'The pace is too fast... It's the co-operation between the dive-bombers and the tanks that is winning the war for Germany'.
- 'News that the Germans are in Amiens [another French town]... this is like some ridiculous nightmare.'

⤴ **SOURCE B:** *From the diary of an unknown French soldier found in 1941. All these diary entries were made between 15 May and 19 May 1940. From www.historylearningsite.co.uk.*

WISE-UP Words
blitzkrieg

What other tactics and strategies are there?
Look through each of the following tactics and strategies – they show some of the key methods used throughout history to defeat enemy forces and win wars.

The fake retreat
The idea here is to pull an enemy away from their strong, well-defended position by pretending to run away (retreat). Then, as enemy soldiers follow your troops, you turn around and attack while they are unprepared. This idea was used by Duke William of Normandy against King Harold of England during the Battle of Hastings in 1066.

SOURCE C: *A painting showing how English foot soldiers were overwhelmed when the Norman knights used the fake retreat tactic against them during the Battle of Hastings.* ↘

Defend, then attack
The idea behind this battleground tactic is simple. First, manoeuvre your army into a great defensive position, for example, one that is high up (so you can see your enemy approaching) and difficult to get behind (so your enemy can't sneak up on you). Then either wait and defend your position, or skilfully attack your enemy time and time again, weakening their forces to the point where they are defeated. This tactic was used by Confederate (Southern) forces when defeating the Union (Northern) troops during the 1862 Battle of Fredericksburg in the American Civil War.

Surprise
The surprise attack has been used throughout history. The idea of waiting for just the right moment to launch a powerful, aggressive and well-planned attack on your enemy has been used for centuries – notably by German tribesmen when wiping out around 10,000 Roman soldiers at the Battle of Teutourg Forest in 9 CE.

Uproar east, attack west

In the late sixth century BCE, a Chinese military general named Sun Tzu wrote a famous book called *The Art of War*, which outlines different tactics used to win wars. Since then, all sorts of military leaders have been inspired by his ideas. One of the many tactics contained in the book is the idea of 'uproar east, attack west'. The plan here is to make the enemy believe you are going to attack in one particular place (uproar east) but to actually attack in another (attack west). This tactic was used with success in 1944, when British and American military planners managed to trick German generals into believing they would attack Nazi-occupied Europe at Calais, France and in Norway – when the real attack would be at Normandy on D-Day!

SOURCE D: *Soldiers lifting up a rubber 'dummy' tank. During World War Two, the British used inflatable tanks to trick German forces into thinking that they were real! This tactic was meant to confuse enemy intelligence (see page 31) and distract attention from the location of the real attack.*

Superior weapons

Many wars have been fought between sides that have more or less the same types of weapons. But on the occasions that one side makes better use of a superior weapon, the results have been devastating for their enemy. At the Battle of Crecy in the Hundred Years War, for example, 12,000 English soldiers fought against 40,000 Frenchmen. But the English had a superior weapon – the longbow. On top of a nearby hill were 2,000 highly trained archers (or longbowmen) who could fire more than 12 arrows each per minute, causing huge casualties to the French forces (see Source E).

'Then the English archers stepped forward one pace and let fly their arrows so together and so thick that it seemed like snow.'

SOURCE E: *A contemporary account of the Battle of Crecy in 1346, written by Jean Froissart.*

Intelligence

When people talk about 'intelligence' during wars and battles, they don't mean how clever someone is. Instead, 'military intelligence' means the collection and analysis of important information about the enemy in order to help military leaders make key decisions. The information may have been gathered by spies or through capturing enemy documents and plans. During World War Two, Polish, French and British code-breakers found out all sorts of information about the movements of German ships, troops and aircraft by capturing German code-books and code machines, and working out what the enemy orders were. This 'intelligence' – according to many historians – played a crucial role in the final defeat of Germany in 1945.

Deception

'Deception' means that you trick (or deceive) your enemy into believing something that isn't true. During World War One, for example, the British Royal Navy fitted ordinary ships with guns and covered them up to disguise them. They were known as Q-Ships after the port in Ireland (Queenstown) where the special ships were fitted out. If a German submarine then surfaced to open fire on what it thought was an ordinary, harmless supply ship bringing food and equipment to the British, the disguise panels dropped away and the guns opened fire! Q-Ships sank or damaged around 70 German submarines in total during World War One.

Penetration

This is one of the oldest – and simplest – military tactics. Here, the attacking army attempts to pierce (or penetrate) the enemy lines so that the enemy soldiers are split into two groups. This then allows the attackers to get in behind them. This was a favourite tactic of the English military commander John Churchill, the Duke of Marlborough, in the early 1700s.

Envelopment

'Enveloping' an enemy basically means 'to surround and encircle' that enemy. If an enemy force is encircled it can be starved of supplies and attacked from all sides. The enemy forces then have only three options: fight their way out, surrender or fight to the death. In 216 BCE a Roman Army of around 60,000 was cut to pieces after being enveloped by Hannibal during the Battle of Cannae. Today, this is viewed as one of the Roman Army's worst defeats.

Work

1 Match the methods, tactics and strategies in List A with the battles, wars or people who used them in List B.

List A	List B
The fake retreat	Battle of Teutourg Forest
Envelopment	Hannibal
Blitzkrieg	Battle of Crecy
Defend, then attack	World War Two code-breakers
Uproar east, attack west	Battle of Hastings
Intelligence	Q-ship campaign
Superior weapons	D-Day
Surprise	Battle of Fredericksburg
Penetration	John Churchill
Deception	Battle for Poland, 1939

2 Look at Sources A and B. In your own words, describe how Blitzkrieg works.

3 Source A is a pictorial explanation of Blitzkrieg. Choose three other methods, tactics or strategies featured on pages 28-31 and create your own pictorial explanation of it.

4 Can you explain the difference between 'strategy' and 'tactics'?

! FACT Strategy and Tactics

Most military experts like to point out the difference between 'military strategy' and 'military tactics'. Put simply, strategy is what you are aiming to do overall, and tactics are the different steps you take to achieve that overall aim. One famous military leader summed it up by saying: 'Tactics is the art of using troops in battle; strategy is the art of using battles to win the war'. So, for example, during World War Two a key *strategy* used by the Allies to beat Germany was to deprive them of fuel for their tanks and aircraft. The *tactic* used to make this happen was a dedicated plan of bombing all the oilfields and refineries under Nazi control.

+ Hungry for MORE

The Art of War is one of the oldest and most successful books on military tactics and strategy in the world. Find out the following about it:
• When was it written? By whom? And why?
• What is each of the main chapters about?
• Who has been influenced by it?

____MISSION ACCOMPLISHED?____

• Could you summarize **three** different tactics or strategies used to win battles or wars?

WAR AND MEDICINE

There is a long, bloody and fascinating relationship between war and medicine. As weapons grew deadlier, doctors, nurses, health services and governments had to work out new ways to cope with the casualties. This Depth Study looks at this relationship in detail, focusing on advances in medicine that were directly linked to warfare, and examining how the treatment of soldiers has changed.

1: The impact of war on medicine

MISSION OBJECTIVES

• To evaluate the significance of Ambroise Paré and Florence Nightingale in the development of medicine during wartime.

Throughout history, one of the key times that the latest medical equipment and techniques are needed is during wartime. If a country's medical services are good then injured soldiers have a better chance of survival. And the more healthy soldiers there are available, the greater a country's chances of victory.

Medicine often develops more quickly during wartime. This is for two reasons:

• Lots of money is spent on medical research and treatment during a war. Governments of fighting countries want soldiers back 'fighting fit' as soon as possible.

• There are more wounded people during wartime. This gives doctors and nurses more opportunities to try out new ideas and techniques.

Read through the following two case studies carefully. They each show how war has had a major impact on our understanding of the body and the way injuries are treated.

CASE STUDY ONE: AMBROISE PARÉ AND THE TREATMENT OF GUNSHOT WOUNDS

Medical treatment has to try and keep up with advances in methods of killing. When swords and spears were replaced by guns and cannons, doctors had to look for ways to treat the gunshot wounds. Ambroise Paré was a French army doctor in the early 1500s. More and more soldiers began staggering into his treatment tent with terrible gunshot wounds. The theory at the time was that gunshot wounds were poisonous – and the only way to stop the poison from spreading around the body was to pour boiling oil on the wound to kill the poison!

One day Paré ran out of oil, so he mixed up an ointment (of egg yolks, oil of roses and turpentine) to put on the gunshot wounds instead. The next morning he found that the men who had been treated with his new ointment were sitting up in bed talking, whilst the men who had been treated with oil were all feverish. As you can imagine, Paré never used boiling oil to treat gunshot wounds again.

But Paré didn't stop there. The usual way of treating a soldier's leg or arm if it had to be amputated was to press a red-hot iron over the stump. The idea was to seal the blood vessels by burning them shut, but many men died from the shock and pain. Paré suggested using silk threads to tie off the blood vessels instead, which was far less painful and a very effective way to stop the bleeding.

Paré eventually published his ideas in a book, which was translated into many languages. His ideas inspired other doctors to try out new techniques and challenge old ideas.

SOURCE A: *Paré's ground-breaking ideas hugely improved the survival rates of wounded soldiers.* ↱

CASE STUDY TWO:
FLORENCE NIGHTINGALE AND NURSING

For thousands of years, women played little part in warfare. Nurses looked after soldiers if they made it to hospital – but many were untrained and badly paid. A woman called Florence Nightingale changed all that!

In 1853, Britain and France went to war with Russia in an area of Eastern Europe called the Crimea. Soon reports got back to Britain of the awful conditions in which injured men were being treated (see Source B). One report said that the sick were dying at an average rate of 80 a day, and hospital ships were packed with hundreds of men with only two doctors and no water to drink!

'In one hospital at Scutari there were over 1000 patients suffering from diarrhoea and only 20 chamber pots to go round. There was an inch of liquid filth covering the floor, and the soldiers had no shoes or socks. Their food was left in the muck. Half of all men suffering from diarrhoea did not survive. There were no screens, so the surgeons amputated the legs of soldiers in front of the rest of them.'

↥ **SOURCE B:** *From a modern history textbook,* Medicine Through the Ages, *by Peter Martin and Richard Pulley (Stanley Thornes, 1990).*

Back in England, a well-educated girl named Florence Nightingale read the horrific reports and decided to do something about it. She took a group of 38 nurses out to the British Army's main hospital in the Crimea. With some money from the government – and some from her own pocket – she rebuilt part of the hospital, scrubbed the floors, boiled the towels and sheets, and provided good food for the patients. The results were amazing! Before Nightingale's arrival around 42% of wounded men died in the hospital – within six months that was down to 2%.

Nightingale returned home a national heroine. She decided that if she could improve hospitals abroad she could do it in Britain too. In 1860 she set up Britain's first nurse training school and within 30 years she had set up schools all over the world. In 1830 there had been no specially trained nurses – 50 years later there were over 7000!

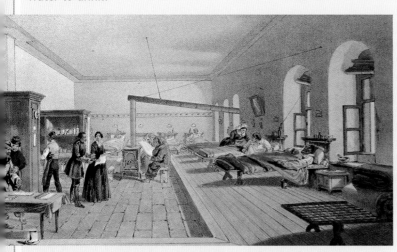

↥ **SOURCE C:** *A picture from 1857 showing Florence Nightingale (in the black dress) in Scutari Hospital in the Crimea. Note the clean floors, warm but ventilated rooms (with windows open), fully stocked medicine cabinets and clean, well spaced beds.*

SOURCE D: *Adapted from an article by M. G. Arnstein, July 1956.* ↴

'All nursing has been influenced by her. You might say that modern nursing is Miss Nightingale. She demonstrated in a dramatic fashion during the Crimean War that nursing could reduce the death rate... Miss Nightingale showed what nursing could do, and more important, established schools to produce people who could do it.'

Work ───────.

1 a Explain why wars often result in major advances and developments in medicine.

b Can you think of reasons why wars might something hinder (hold back) medical progress?

2 Prepare a fact-file each for Ambroise Paré and Florence Nightingale, containing four sections:
- What did they do?
- Why did they do it?
- Why were they important in the short-term?
- Why were they important in the long-term?

Note: Before starting your fact-files, you may want to define the key differences between long and short term.

! FACT Not all progress?

Some people have argued that wars can actually slow down medical progress rather than speeding it up. After all, thousands of doctors are taken away from their normal work to treat injured soldiers, rather than continuing with their medical research.

── **MISSION ACCOMPLISHED?** ──

- Can you explain how Ambroise Paré and Florence Nightingale made both a short and long-term impact on medicine?

There have been two World Wars. Both were global conflicts that killed and wounded millions more people than any wars before them. New and deadly weapons – like high explosive shells, gas, flamethrowers and machine guns – were used on a massive scale for the first time and inflicted horrific injuries. Over 10 million people were killed in World War One (1914–1918) and over 20 million died in World War Two (1939–1945). There were also many millions more who were injured – wars always tend to wound more soldiers than they kill. Yet despite the great suffering caused by these two terrible wars, a number of improvements in health and medicine were made as a result.

2: How did two World Wars change medicine?

MISSION OBJECTIVES

- To remember at least **two** examples of medical progress that resulted from World War One, and **two** examples that resulted from World War Two.

What was the impact of World War One on medicine?

During wartime, doctors and scientists work hard on medical ideas and techniques that increase soldiers' chances of survival. During World War One there were several key developments that changed medical care. Some of these may have happened anyway, but World War One sped them up because there was such an urgent need to help injured soldiers. For example, scientists had been working on ways to give blood transfusions for years, but the amount of injured soldiers needing them in World War One meant that scientists worked even harder and faster to make transfusions possible. X-rays had also been around for about 20 years by 1914, but the huge number of soldiers requiring X-rays in the war accelerated the pace of development and improvement of the technique.

Plastic surgery
World War One saw the first ever use of what we now call 'plastic surgery' to repair soldiers' injured faces. A doctor named Harold Gillies set up a special unit to **graft** (surgically attach) skin onto men who had suffered severe facial wounds. He continued his work after the war and by 1921 over 5000 soldiers, sailors and airmen had been treated.

X-rays
The ability to take X-rays had been around since 1895, but it was during World War One that the technology became really widespread. Mobile X-ray machines were used to find out exactly where bullets or pieces of shrapnel were lodged in soldiers' bodies.

Shell shock

The mental strain of war could cause a condition known as 'shell shock'. The traumatic sights they witnessed and the constant fear of sudden and violent death led to lots of soldiers suffering panic attacks, physically trembling all the time, or being unable to speak or move. Initially the army refused to recognize the condition and treated the shell-shocked soldiers as cowards. However, by the end of the war there were so many cases that 'shell shock' became an officially recognized medical condition. Today, the condition is known as PTSD (post-traumatic stress disorder) or CSR (combat stress reaction).

Broken bones

New techniques were developed during World War One to repair broken bones. The 'army leg splint', for example, elevated the leg 'in traction', which helped the bones to knit together better. This technique is still used today.

Work

1 Why, during World War One, did doctors, surgeons and scientists need to work very hard on developing and improving medical ideas and techniques?

2 Imagine you are an army doctor, surgeon or nurse during World War One. Write a short letter home to your friends and family explaining how the latest scientific and technological developments have helped you in your work.

Artificial limbs

Between 1914 and 1921, more than 41,000 British men lost at least one limb as a result of their war injuries. This huge number of amputees meant that hospitals like Queen Mary's in Roehampton began to work hard to create comfortable, strong and light artificial limbs. By 1918 new and improved materials were increasingly being used and new ways to make the artificial limbs bend better were invented.

Blood transfusions

During World War One scientists worked tirelessly to find ways to store blood properly so that soldiers who had lost a lot of blood could have it replaced (transfused) quickly. In 1914 new techniques stopped the blood clotting, and by 1917 blood could be bottled, packed in ice and taken to where it was needed by surgeons operating on soldiers. The ability to store blood in advance allowed the first Blood Bank (which still exists today) to be set up in 1937.

What was the impact of World War Two on medicine?

The medical situation in World War Two was similar to that in World War One. The millions of wounded soldiers meant that doctors, surgeons and scientists worldwide worked even harder to develop new medicines and techniques – and they also tried to improve on some of the advances made earlier.

Heart surgery

Heart surgery progressed significantly during World War Two. American army surgeon Dwight Harken cut into beating hearts and used his bare hands to remove bits of shrapnel and bullets. His findings helped heart surgery to continue developing rapidly after the war.

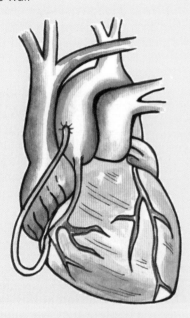

Plastic surgery

A doctor from New Zealand named Archibald McIndoe (who was a cousin of Harold Gillies – see the pages on medicine in World War One) used new drugs to prevent infection when treating pilots with horrific burns. His work in rebuilding damaged faces and hands was respected (and copied) all over the world.

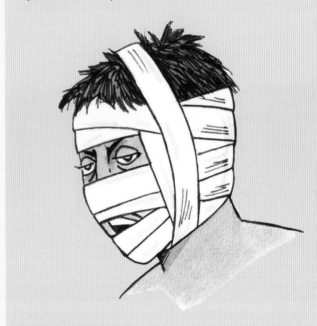

Drug development

Penicillin, the first mass-produced **antibiotic**, was first developed in the years leading up to World War Two. It was used during the war by the Americans and British to cure infections in deep wounds.

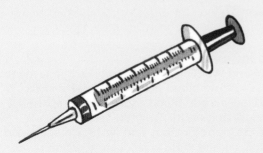

The National Health Service

During the war, politicians began to plan how health care could be organized better once the fighting was over. In 1942, a government worker named William Beveridge proposed a 'free National Health Service for all'. Just after the war finished, the government put his plans into action and the NHS was born.

Hygiene, disease and diet

In order to try and keep Britain 'fighting fit', posters were produced during World War Two encouraging people to stay healthy. They warned against the dangers of poor hygiene. A national immunization programme against killer diseases like **diphtheria** was launched too, and people were encouraged to grow their own food because there were national shortages of some foods. Much of the food that people grew in their own back gardens or allotments was fruit and vegetables – which was very healthy!

Blood transfusions

Large blood banks were developed in both the USA and Britain during World War Two, much of it donated by civilians. This blood saved countless lives by helping to treat injured soldiers. In 1946, Britain launched its National Blood Service.

❚❚ PAUSE for Thought

What do you think are the main reasons why some people argue that war can hinder (hold up) the development of medicine and medical treatment?

➕ Hungry for MORE

Try to find out how the National Health Service has developed over the years. When did it start up? What services did it first offer? How has it changed over the years? How is it paid for? How has it affected you and your family's lives?

WISE-UP Words

antibiotic

diphtheria

graft

transfusion

Work ⌇⌇⌇⌇⌇.

1 a What, in your opinion, are the main differences between 'health' and 'medicine'?
  b List ways in which war has affected:
  i health
  ii medicine
  c Which of these effects do you think was the most important?

2 Of the developments featured here, and those on pages 34 and 35, which do you think:
  i would **not** have happened if it wasn't for war?
  ii would have happened anyway, but were sped up by war?

3 Have **you** personally been affected by any of the advances and developments brought about by war? For example, have you ever been treated with the antibiotic, penicillin?

4 'War leads and medicine follows'. What do you think this means, and do you agree with it? Support your answer with examples and evidence wherever possible.

⎯ MISSION ACCOMPLISHED? ⎯

• Can you describe **two** medical advances made during World War One, and **two** made during World War Two?

DEPTH STUDY
WAR AND MEDICINE

The risk of losing a limb has been ever-present on the battlefield throughout history. Swords, axes, cannonballs, artillery shells, hand grenades and dozens of other weapons had the potential to **sever** an arm or blow off a leg. So how has one of warfare's most horrific injuries been treated at different times in history?

3: A history of losing a limb

_____ MISSION OBJECTIVES _____

• To compare and contrast how major injuries on the battlefield have been dealt with by medical staff since Roman times.

Read the following stories of four front-line soldiers from different eras of warfare to see how they got their injuries, the medical attention they received, and how they were treated when their fighting careers ended.

Titus Septimius Scaro was a Roman legionary based in Londinium in the furthest outpost of the Roman Empire – Britannia. In CE61 Titus's leg was cut very badly and both its bones were broken below the knee in a battle with **Iceni** tribesmen near Verulamium (St Albans).

Titus waited on the battlefield in agony until the battle was over, and then he was taken back to camp.

Surgeons tried to stop the bleeding using a leather **tourniquet** and the main arteries were 'tied off'. He was given poppy seeds and wine to sedate him.

The wound was cleaned with vinegar, wine and honey. Some surgeons stuffed cuts with snails and animal dung too!

After a few days gangrene set in and the army surgeons agreed that the leg must be amputated just below the knee. There was no anaesthetic.

Some healthy flesh was cut away to ensure no gangrene remained. The stump was covered in turpentine and pitch to prevent further infection.

Titus survived and was taken back to the Valetudinarium (hospital) in Londinium. He returned to Rome soon after.

Titus's army career was over. As he was near the end of his 25-year service, he was given land and money… and permission to marry!

Thomas Atkyns fought in the navy for England's Queen Elizabeth against Spain in 1588. During the battle of Gravelines in August 1588, Thomas's right shoulder was hit as Spanish cannonballs smashed through his ship.

WISE-UP Words

cauterize

Iceni

sever

tourniquet

His right arm was also hit by several musket-balls fired by Spanish riflemen onboard a nearby galleon.

Thomas had to wait below deck until the battle ended. There was no doctor on board but his shipmates bound his arm tightly to try to stop the bleeding.

He was given alcohol to dull the intense pain, and when he eventually got back to port he was taken to a surgeon.

The surgeon saw that infection had set in, so he amputated Thomas's smashed arm above the elbow.

A hot iron was used to **cauterize** the wound (burn the blood vessels to seal them)... but Thomas had lost too much blood and died three days later.

It was a shame Thomas wasn't treated by Ambroise Paré, a French surgeon. He tied off blood vessels with silk thread rather than cauterizing them.

Paré dressed wounds with turpentine, rose oil and egg yolk. His patients had a far better survival rate and he even designed artificial limbs for them!

Arthur Lindop was an infantry soldier with the Devonshire Regiment during the Great War. He went 'over the top' on the first day of the war's largest battle, the Battle of the Somme (July to November 1916). Arthur's leg was shattered when a hand grenade exploded next to him. Stretcher bearers carried him off the battlefield during a break in the fighting.

They bandaged his wounds and gave him morphine for the pain. He was moved to a field hospital in a horse-drawn ambulance.

Infection was prevented using an antiseptic treatment called Dakin's Fluid, but Arthur's injuries were beyond repair so the surgeon had to amputate.

Arthur was given an anaesthetic during the operation and pain relief when he woke up. The leg was treated again with antiseptic to stop infection.

Arthur was later fitted with an artificial leg at St Mary's Hospital, Roehampton.

He received a small disabled serviceman's war pension, but it wasn't really enough for his family to survive on.

In 1923 Arthur got a job at a factory in Richmond, making artificial poppies that were sold to make money to help other disabled war veterans.

THE POPPY FACTORY
RICHMOND UPON THAMES
EST. 1922
by MAJOR GEORGE HOWSON

The original poppy was designed so that workers with war disabilities could easily assemble it. Today, the Poppy Appeal raises millions each year.

Corporal Steven Tompkins was serving with the 3rd Battalion, the Parachute Regiment in the Helmand Province of Afghanistan in September 2006. Whilst out on a routine patrol, a landmine detonated below his right foot.

His right foot was blown off, he suffered deep gashes to his thighs and he also lost two fingers on his right hand.

Within an hour a Chinook helicopter had airlifted Steven to a field hospital in the nearby town of Helmand.

He received top medical care in a state of the art army hospital. Later, when one of the wounds got infected, it was treated with antibiotics.

A few weeks later, Steven was moved to Selly Oak Hospital in Birmingham. He later went to the army's specialist rehabilitation centre in Surrey.

Steven was fitted with an artificial leg (called a prosthetic) made from strong, lightweight materials such as plastic and carbon fibre.

Steven received a lump sum payment and an army pension based on his last year's earnings. He hopes to retrain for a career in teaching.

Some disabled people continue to serve in the military, but most leave. Some feel that veterans don't receive the support they deserve for their sacrifices.

Work

1 Can you think of reasons why so much time and effort goes into the treatment of wounded soldiers?

2 Copy out the chart that has been started to the right and add a column for each of the other wounded soldiers in the stories. Then fill in your chart using the information from each of the four soldiers' tales.

3 Choose **two** of the following areas and use the stories to write a paragraph or two explaining how they have developed over the last 2000 years:
   • pain relief
   • amputation surgery
   • artificial limbs

Name	Titus Septimus Scaro
Injury	
Cause of injury	
Was he taken off the battlefield soon after being injured? Give details	
How quickly did he receive treatment, and where?	
Was he given anything to numb the pain? If so, what? If not, can you think why?	
How was he treated immediately after amputation?	
By today's standards, rate the medical care and attention he received, 10 being excellent, 1 being poor	

✚ Hungry for MORE

Choose another period in history and research how 'losing a limb' was treated at that time. You might want to create a series of cartoons to go with your research. You could choose the Bronze Age, the early Middle Ages around 1066, the Napoleonic Wars, World War Two, or the Vietnam War, for example.

__MISSION ACCOMPLISHED?__

• Can you explain **five** key changes in the way medics have dealt with major injuries over the last 2000 years?

Have you been learning? 1

TASK 1 Spot the mistakes

a Can you suggest reasons why medicine usually develops at a greater rate during wartime than in peacetime?

b Below are eight paragraphs about key medical developments made during wartime. Each paragraph has two errors. One is a spelling mistake; the other is a factual error. When you have spotted the mistakes, write the sentences out correctly.

1 Ambroise Paré, a young Spanish doctor working with the French Army, made great advances in the treetment of amputations and saved many lives by treating gunshot wounds with soothing ointments rather than hot oil.

2 Florence Nightingale worked as a nurse during World War One. She saved hundreds of lives by insisting on good higiene in the military hospital at Scutari, and when she came back to Britain she set up the world's first training school for nurses.

3 During the Great War of 1914 to 1919, mobile X-ray machines were used to find out exactly where bullets or pieces of shrapnel were lodged in soldiers' bodys.

4 Over 41,000 British men lost a limb during the Great War. The latest tecnology was used to make artificial arms and legs at Queen David's Hospital in Roehampton and this allowed wounded soldiers to lead much more comfortable lives.

5 In 1914 new techniques where found that stopped blood from clotting. By 1917, blood could be bottled, packed in straw and taken to where it was needed by surgeons operating on soldiers.

6 Plastic surgery was first used during the Great War when a doctor named Harold Gillies set up a special unit to treat men suffering from severe facial wounds. By 1921, over 50 soliders, sailors and airmen had been treated.

7 Penicillen was the first mass-produced antibiotic. It was used by British and German troops during World War Two to cure infections.

8 Large blood banks were developed in both Britain and the USA during World War Two. In 1936, the National Blood Service was launched in Britain, which still campains for people to 'Give Blood' today.

c There is little doubt that some of the developments outlined here have had a positive effect on people's health in today's world. Have any of these wartime medical developments had an impact on your life or on the lives of your family members? Give examples if you can.

TASK 2 Types of war anagrams

Use the following clues to unscramble the anagrams in the list below.

• A war fought between different groups within the same country.

• A war fought in different places around the world by countries from all over the world.

• A type of war in which a group within a country rises up in an attempt to get rid of the ruling group.

• A war in which nuclear weapons are the main weapon.

• A war in which major countries don't actually fight, but get involved by taking different sides in a smaller conflict.

• A type of war where religious beliefs play a major role.

• A war where small groups stage surprise attacks, ambushes and raids on occupying forces.

RAIVWLIC

OWLRARWD

YOURLOTRAVEWINAR

NEARRAWLUC

WRAPOXRY

LEGROOFINRIAW

LAWRAGELIRU

TASK 3 Find it!

Copy this puzzle into your book or on a sheet of paper. Be careful to draw all your boxes in the correct places or you won't be able to find the final word.

Fill in the answers to the clues.

Then read down the puzzle (clue 10). Write a paragraph explaining the impact this invention had on weapons and warfare.

Clues:

1. Could fire an arrow over 200 metres

2. An early type of gun

3. First used during World War One

4. A war machine for throwing rocks

5. Could fire sharp bolts through armour

6. An ancient hand-held weapon

7. A small bomb thrown by hand

8. _____ ram

9. Men fighting on horseback

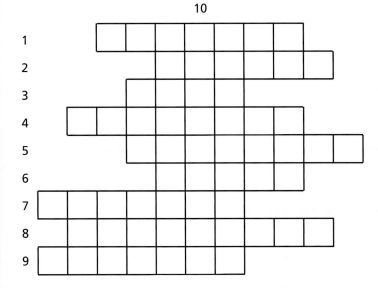

TASK 4 Propaganda: Influencing the wartime population

Propaganda means spreading ideas and opinions. The aim is to influence people and to get them to believe certain things, even if you have to tell them lies! All governments do this in wartime. They try to get people to think what they want them to think. During World War Two, for example, news reports were censored and newspapers only published what they were told. News of battle defeats hardly got a mention whilst even relatively small victories were reported as major triumphs. Sometimes news was even kept secret because it could help the enemy - weather reports, for example, were stopped during the war because it was thought that if the Germans knew about weather conditions in Britain it might help them with their invasion plans!

a Write a detailed definition of the word 'propaganda'.

b Read the propaganda stories below about alleged German atrocities (cruel acts that broke the 'rules' of war) during World War Two.

> French children were machine-gunned by German soldiers when they conquered France. Their mothers were killed too.

> German prison camp guards refused to give captured and wounded soldiers any medical treatment or water.

> Priests all over Belgium and Holland who refused to ring their church bells to celebrate the Germans taking their town were killed and hung on the bells.

i) Explain how you think propaganda could be used as another weapon of war. Think about how reading these stories in a newspaper would make people feel about Germany, for example.

ii) Based on what you have read above, write your own short propaganda newspaper story. It could be from World War Two, like the stories above, or based on the events of another war you have studied.

Can war ever be justified?

―――――――― MISSION OBJECTIVES ――――――――

• To be able to outline the key arguments for and against the use of war.

Whenever a country gets involved in a war, there is often a key question debated in homes and workplaces, in the newspapers and on the television and radio: should we have gone to war? In Britain, for example, every major conflict involving British troops sees a national debate on the arguments for and against war. During these debates you hear all sorts of views from all sorts of people – from those who support the use of war in certain situations, to those who think that no war, no matter what, can ever be justified.

This double page aims to summarize some of the most common views and opinions on the question 'can war ever be justified?'

Ⓐ Life is sacred. The value of human life – any human life, even that of your enemy – is so high that nothing can justify killing another human being on purpose.

Ⓑ War *is* justified when it is waged against an evil leader or government. It is right to fight wars to get rid of men like Hitler, or to end slavery, or to stop a leader from murdering thousands of innocent people.

Ⓒ The problem with war, any war, is that it also leads to the deaths of innocent people – and that's wrong. Wars are started by politicians, kings and queens... but it's the ordinary people who fight and die in them. It just isn't fair!

Ⓓ If 100,000 people have to die in a war in order to save the lives of 20 or 30 million people, then that's a reasonable cost... isn't it?

Ⓔ War is *not* always wrong. It is totally justified if you defend yourself against an invading army. Governments have a duty to use war in order to protect their citizens.

F The reason why no war today can be justified is that the future of the human race is at risk if a fighting nation gets hold of nuclear weapons and uses them!

G I believe in the 'Just War Theory'. It says that war is acceptable only if it is used as a last resort when all other options have been tried, and it is used to put right something that is wrong. War should only be declared by a lawful authority like a government in a democratic country. And civilians should never be targets.

WISE-UP Words

pacifist

Work

1 **a** Write down a definition of the term 'justified'.

   b Make two lists using the opinions (A-J) on these pages. The first list should feature all those opinions that state that war can never be justified. The second list should include the opinions that say that war can be justified at certain times and in certain situations.

2 Work with a partner to create a conversation between two people – one who believes that it is sometimes right for countries to fight, and the other who thinks that war can never be justified. What are the main points of the conversation? What do you disagree over most? Do you agree about anything?

H War isn't actually necessary. Look at Gandhi in India in the 1930s – he defeated the British without ever resorting to violence. His campaign of peaceful protest, not violence, eventually worked.

I Being 'against war' *sounds* great – but in the real world it's hard to stick with that opinion. It's OK if no-one wants to attack your country, but if a whole country took a **pacifist** view, you can bet that country would soon be conquered.

✚ Hungry for MORE

Divide the class into two groups – one group that thinks that war can never be justified, and another that thinks that it can. In your group, discuss ways to present your argument. Research your view, backing it up with evidence – figures, details and examples. Why not present your side of the argument as a Powerpoint, poster or leaflet? Then, as a whole class, hold a debate called 'Can war ever be justified?'

J There are certain times when war can be justified. Take France in 1940. In the years up to 1940, the Nazis had been viciously mistreating Jews, gypsies, disabled people and political opponents not only in Germany, but in all the countries they conquered. In 1940 the Nazis invaded France – and the French Army fought back. Nobody can say that wasn't justified. The French were right to try and resist the Nazis.

MISSION ACCOMPLISHED?

• Would you be able to present a balanced argument of views for and against war?

THE WORLD AT WAR

There have been two conflicts that have been labelled as 'World Wars'. The first one lasted just over four years, between August 1914 and November 1918. The second started 21 years later in September 1939 and lasted nearly six years, until August 1945. This Depth Study aims to analyse these two conflicts in detail, looking at why they are called *World* Wars, how they compare in terms of causes, technology and people involved, and what impact they had on the civilian populations of some of the key fighting nations, particularly Britain.

1: What is a 'World War'?

MISSION OBJECTIVES
• To demonstrate that you know what makes a 'World War' different from other types of war.

Sadly, war is a common occurrence. For thousands of years, groups of people have fought against other groups. Usually these wars were fought on a small scale between just a few different tribes or countries. But around 100 years ago, in 1914, a war began that involved over 70 million military personnel. They came from many of the world's most powerful countries and the fighting took place in various different parts of the world. This soon became known as 'The Great War' or 'World War' because of the sheer scale of the conflict.

World War

There is no clear definition of what makes a 'World War', but most experts agree that for a war to get this label it needs to affect the majority of the world's most powerful and populated countries. World Wars are about conflict on a large scale – they involve multiple countries, on multiple continents, with battles fought in a wide variety of geographical areas and conditions… and they last for years! The label has usually been applied to two conflicts that took place within a few decades of each other in the twentieth century – the Great War of 1914–1918 (also known as World War One or the First World War) and World War Two (or the Second World War), which lasted from 1939 to 1945 (see Sources A and B).

SOURCE A: *A map showing the countries involved in the Great War (1914–1918) and the main theatres of war (areas where the actual fighting took place). Over 100 countries were involved in total, from Africa, America, Asia, Australia and Europe. Some countries* **mobilized** *millions of soldiers and fought for the full length of the war (like Britain, France and Germany), whilst other nations declared war towards the end when they thought they knew which side would come out on top. Some countries (like India, Australia and Jamaica) were drawn into it because they were part of the British Empire and wanted to support the 'mother country'.* ↱

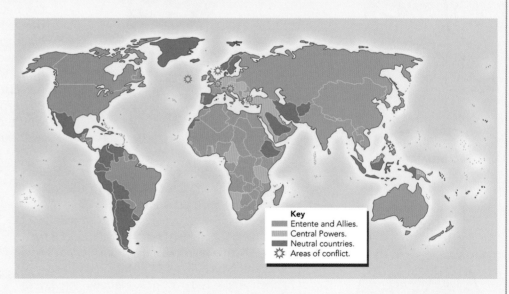

Key
Entente and Allies.
Central Powers.
Neutral countries.
☼ Areas of conflict.

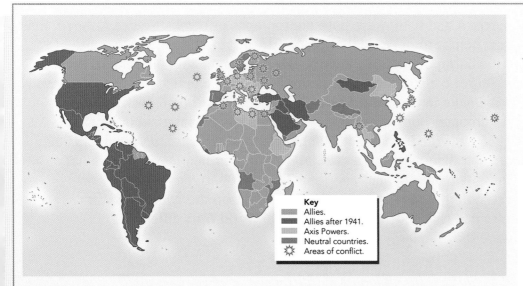

Key
Allies.
Allies after 1941.
Axis Powers.
Neutral countries.
✹ Areas of conflict.

↳ **SOURCE B:** *A map showing the countries involved in World War Two (1939–1945) and the theatres of war. As you can see, this was another global conflict that was in fact the most widespread in history, with more than 100 million military personnel involved from nearly all of the world's major nations.*

Only two World Wars?

Experts have argued for a long time that there have been other conflicts that perhaps also deserve the label of 'World War'. For example, Winston Churchill (Britain's leader in World War Two) called the Seven Years War of 1756–1763 'the First World War' in a history book he wrote. Source C shows the countries involved in that particular conflict. Also, the Napoleonic Wars of 1803–1815, which ended with Napoleon's defeat at Waterloo, have been labelled a 'global conflict' too, because they involved lots of different nations (the UK, Austria, Russia, France, Spain, Holland and many more) in various different parts of the world. Indeed, at the time, the Napoleonic Wars were known as 'the Great War'.

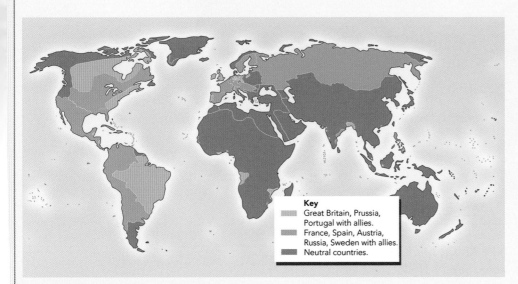

Key
Great Britain, Prussia, Portugal with allies.
France, Spain, Austria, Russia, Sweden with allies.
Neutral countries.

↳ **SOURCE C:** *Participants of the Seven Years War (1756–1763) – a conflict that Winston Churchill called 'the First World War'.*

⭐ WISE-UP Words

mobilize

theatres of war

Work ﹏﹏﹏﹏.

1 When, exactly, were World War One and Two?

2 Why do you think historians refer to these conflicts as 'World Wars'?

3 **a** What is the difference between 'compare' and 'contrast'?
  b Using Sources A and B (and their labels), compare and contrast World War One and World War Two. Think about which countries were involved and where the fighting took place.

4 Why do you think World Wars are far better known, more easily remembered, and studied more than almost any other war?

5 Why do you think some people, including Winston Churchill, refer to the Seven Years War as a 'World War'? Give reasons for your answer.

❗ FACT Who, what, when?

The term 'World War' was first used before 1914 when a writer described a war that might break out in the future! The term 'First World War' was first used to describe the conflict of 1914–1918 in 1933, but many people continued to call it the 'Great War' instead. The term 'World War Two' was first used in 1939 when the conflict began.

___ MISSION ACCOMPLISHED? ___

• In no more than 50 words, can you summarize what is meant by the term 'World War'?

Look at Sources A and B. They are both photographs of bombs. Source A shows one of the largest bombs from World War One (1914–1918). The artillery gun used to fire it is in the background. Upon impact, this weapon might kill or injure dozens of soldiers. Source B also shows a large bomb, but this one is from World War Two (1939–1945). Unlike the bomb in Source A, it is a nuclear bomb. Nicknamed 'Fat Man', it was dropped from an aeroplane onto the city of Nagasaki in Japan on 9 August 1945 and killed around 40,000 people in a split second. Around 25,000 were injured and thousands more died later from their injuries or from radiation sickness. These two bombs, built less than 30 years apart, demonstrate how weapons technology had changed in the time between the two World Wars. But what else had changed? How were the two World Wars different… and how were they similar?

2: How do the two World Wars compare?

————————————— MISSION OBJECTIVES —————————————

• To identify three key aspects of each World War and assess how they compare.

Study the following groups of sources carefully. They each focus on a different aspect of the two World Wars. You will be asked to look for any similarities and differences that the sources show, and to explain which aspects of the war you think changed the most and the least from World War One to World War Two.

↵ **SOURCE A:** *A German shell from the Great War, 1914–1918.*

SOURCE B: *'Fat Man', pictured here in 1945, is one of only two nuclear bombs ever used in warfare.* ↱

How many were killed?

SOURCE C: *Military and civilian deaths in World Wars One and Two for some of the main fighting nations. Note that the axes have different scales and that the total number of casualties in World War Two was many times greater than in World War One. What else can we learn from these graphs about the death tolls of World Wars One and Two?*

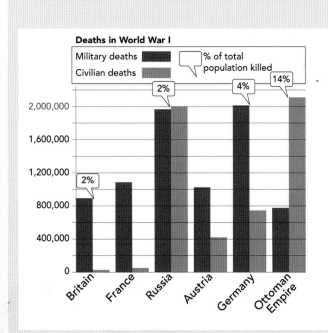

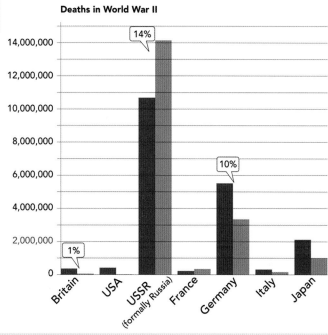

What about air power?

SOURCE D: *One of World War One's most successful fighter planes – the Sopwith Camel. Over 5400 were made. They were equipped with two machine guns, could reach a height of 6400 metres and had a top speed of 115 miles per hour. They had a range of 300 miles.*

SOURCE E: *One of World War Two's most successful fighter planes – the Hawker Hurricane. Over 14,500 were made. They were equipped with eight machine guns and two bombs. They could reach a height of 10,970 metres, had a top speed of 340 miles per hour and a range of 600 miles.*

How powerful were the tanks?

SOURCE F: *Tanks were first used in warfare by the British in 1916. They were equipped with six machine guns and could reach a top speed of 4 miles per hour. Their armour was 6–12mm thick.*

SOURCE G: *One of the most famous tanks of World War Two, the German-made Panzer. Each one was equipped with a cannon that fired high explosive shells and two or three machine guns. Their armour was 80mm thick and they could reach a top speed of around 26 miles per hour.*

How did sea power compare?

SOURCE H: *The British Super Dreadnought class of battleship was the best known of World War One. Reaching speeds of 24 knots (44km/h) and with a range of 5000 miles, these ships were equipped with eight large guns or cannons and 22 other guns. They also had four tubes to fire torpedoes. The armour was around 12 inches (30cm) thick.*

SOURCE I: *The American-made Iowa class battleship of World War Two. Reaching speeds of 31 knots (57km/h) and with a range of 15,000 miles, these ships were equipped with nine large guns and 20 smaller guns. They also had around 120 anti-aircraft machine guns on board. The armour was around 12 inches thick and they carried three small aircraft too!*

What was the fighting like?

SOURCE J: *World War One was a static war, fought from lines of trenches. Attacks by soldiers leaving these trenches were supported by artillery and machine guns, early aeroplanes and poison gas.*

SOURCE K: *World War Two was mainly a war of speed and movement. Tanks and submarines played a significant part and fighting was done on open plains and in towns and cities. Nuclear bombs and rocket-powered missiles were both used.*

How did the destruction compare?

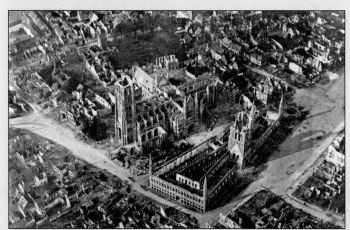

SOURCE L: *The Belgian town of Ypres, pictured in September 1915.*

SOURCE M: *The French town of Saint Lo, pictured in August 1944.*

Work

1 Work in pairs or small groups:
Either: Create a diagram or poster that sums up the SIMILARITIES and DIFFERENCES between World War One and World War Two. Think about the following categories:
- the death toll
- air power
- land power
- naval power
- fighting
- destruction

Or: Prepare a presentation which compares the two World Wars. Make sure you cover the same categories above.

2 Now write two paragraphs. The first paragraph should explain in what ways you think that war changed most from World War One to World War Two. The second should explain in what ways you think that war changed least.

MISSION ACCOMPLISHED?

- Can you outline **three** ways in which World War One differed from World War Two... and any ways that they were similar?

World Wars One and Two did not just involve soldiers, sailors and airmen. The armed forces may have been the ones who went off to fight the enemy on foreign soil, but the people left at home had their part to play too. So what impact did the wars have on people on the **home front**?

3: How did the World Wars affect ordinary citizens?

MISSION OBJECTIVES

- To identify **five** ways in which World War One affected ordinary citizens.
- To identify **five** ways in which World War Two affected ordinary citizens.

Study the two cartoons on the following pages carefully. The impact of the World Wars is seen through the eyes of two children, one from World War One (on these pages) and one from World War Two (on pages 54 and 55).

The Germans flew huge inflatable airships – called **Zeppelins** – over Britain and used them to bomb British towns. By the end of the war over 50 Zeppelin air raids had dropped over 5000 bombs, killing 557 people and injuring over 1300. German bomber planes attacked Britain too, and German battleships shelled seaside towns.

When war broke out the government introduced a new law called the 'Defence of the Realm Act' or DORA. It gave the government the power to do whatever it felt was necessary to win the war. They could take over mines, railways and shipyards, and control newspapers and radio. To limit drunken behaviour, for example, they introduced strict pub opening hours… and even allowed beer to be watered down!

Around 70 million men fought in World War One, with over 8 million of these fighting for Britain and its Empire. Nearly one million of those were killed and twice as many were injured. By the end of the war, it was estimated that there were only 12 towns or villages in Britain that hadn't lost a young man in the fighting. By 1916, Britain was so short of soldiers that they introduced **conscription** for men aged between 18 and 41. This meant that if you were selected you had to fight by law.

In the early days of the war, women were encouraged to pin white feathers (a sign of cowardice) on young men who weren't in an army uniform. The idea was to shame them into 'doing their bit' in the war.

With so many men away fighting, women were needed to do their jobs. Before the war, no one would have dreamed of having female bus drivers, chimney sweeps or steel makers, but now Britain needed them! Thousands of women found work in shipyards, in weapons factories and with the ambulance service. And for the first time, the government recruited women into the police force!

Work

1 What is meant by the term 'home front'?

2 What was DORA and why do you think the British government thought it was necessary?

3 a Why did the British government introduce conscription?

   b Before conscription, how do you think the government got men to fight? Make a list of all the methods they could have used.

4 How did World War One change the role of women? Don't just think about jobs, think about their role in the family.

Britain was short of food in the war because German submarines and battleships were sinking the boats that brought it by sea. So the government introduced **rationing** to make sure that food was equally shared out. Each person was allowed a set amount of butter, sugar, bacon, ham, and so on.

During the war, some goods were in short supply – so prices went up. The government also had to borrow millions from the USA to pay for the war, so taxes went up to pay back the loans.

How were ordinary citizens affected by World War Two?

The Germans tried to cut off supplies of food and other goods by sinking the ships that brought the supplies to Britain. So, in 1940, the government introduced rationing. This meant that every person was entitled to a fixed weekly amount of fuel, clothing and certain types of food. The government also encouraged people to grow their own food in their back gardens or allotments. The slogan for the campaign was 'Dig for Victory'.

When the war began, everyone expected to be bombed from the air – so civilians prepared for it. Millions of people built their own bomb shelters in their back gardens.

Air Raid Precaution (ARP) Wardens had the job of patrolling the streets at night to make sure that no light was visible and helping out if there was an air raid. There were 1.4 million ARP Wardens altogether, many of them part-time volunteers who also worked full-time during the day.

In May 1940 the government urged all men aged between 17 and 65 who weren't in the army to join the 'Home Guard'. Their role was to work part-time in their local area and prepare it for attack. Many of the men in the Home Guard were not permitted to join the regular army because their jobs were necessary to the war effort – farm workers, teachers, grocers, bank workers and railwaymen, for example. Others were too old to join up or had health problems. They weren't paid and to begin with they didn't have any weapons… so some made their own!

In late 1940 German bombers began to bomb Britain's major cities. This was known as 'The Blitz'. Swansea, Cardiff, Bristol, Southampton, Plymouth, Birmingham, Coventry, Liverpool, Glasgow, Manchester, Sunderland, Aberdeen, Sheffield and many other cities were targeted. London suffered the heaviest bombing – for one 11-week period, London was bombed every night except one! By the end of May 1941, over 30,000 civilians had been killed in the bombing raids and 87,000 were seriously injured. In London alone, over one million homes were destroyed or damaged.

People put up thick curtains that they could shut at night-time to prevent any glimmer of light from escaping and helping enemy bombers to locate their target. Street lights were switched off or dimmed too, and cars were fitted with masked headlights. Windows were taped to stop glass from shattering all over the place if a bomb exploded nearby.

Britain was organized like never before during World War Two. The government had the power to move people to any job they felt necessary to help win the war. Millions of women worked in weapons factories, on farms and in army, navy and air force bases. Single women were forced to work but married women weren't. However, many decided to work anyway while looking after their families as well.

Work

1 Imagine you were the child pictured in the cartoon on this page. Write a letter to your father, who is away fighting, about how World War Two has changed life in Britain and your family life at home. You may wish to include details about:

- the Blitz
- air raid precautions
- evacuation
- changing roles of women
- the Home Guard
- rationing
- the Dig for Victory campaign
- your own family's contribution to the war.

KEEP CLEAR UNEXPLODED BOMB

When war broke out, the government was worried that large British cities would be targets for aircraft bombing raids. So schoolchildren (and their teachers) were evacuated from the cities that were considered to be in danger – London, Birmingham, Coventry, Bristol, Portsmouth, Glasgow, etc. Pregnant women, blind and disabled people, and women with children under five were also sent by road and train to safer countryside areas.

The government issued millions of gas masks to civilians as a precaution against gas bombs.

MISSION ACCOMPLISHED?

- Are you able to recall the main ways in which each World War affected children, women, family life, food, and so on?

How much do wars cost?

MISSION OBJECTIVES

• To be able to differentiate between the different types of 'costs' involved in war.

Wars are expensive. Very, very expensive. And it's not just the guns, bullets, tanks, planes and battleships that cost a lot of money. There's the cost of actually paying the soldiers, running the training bases, and buying all the food, clothes and fuel that a modern army needs. And there's another cost involved in warfare too – the cost in human lives and injuries.

What do weapons cost?

Governments spend billions on their armed forces each year. The UK, for example, one of the world's top five 'big spenders' in military terms, spends around £35 billion every year. China spends around £70 billion whilst India spends about £17 billion. The USA (the biggest spender of all) spends around nine times more than the UK. To put this into perspective, however, the £35 billion spent on the UK's armed forces is considerably less than it spends on education (around £75 billion) and healthcare (around £110 billion).

SOURCE A: *Some of the biggest-selling weapons used by armed forces all over the world and their approximate prices. To put these prices into perspective, a general hospital costs around £100 million to build and an average secondary school costs between £8 million and £20 million!* ↷

Weapon	Cost	Made by
Aircraft carrier	£1 billion	BAE Systems, UK
B2 Stealth Bomber	£600 million	Northrop Grumman, USA
F-15 Attack Fighter	£60 million	Boeing, USA
AH-64 Apache Attack Helicopter	£30 million	Boeing, USA
Sukhoi S-30 Fighter	£12 million	Sukhoi, Russia
Tomahawk Block 111C Cruise Missile	£600,000	Raytheon, USA
Cluster Bomb RBL 755	£5,000	INSYS, UK
AK-47 Kalashnikov	£400	Izhmash, Russia
M16 Rifle	£400	Colt, USA

Does spending increase during a war?

When countries go to war the amount they spend on their armed forces increases dramatically, because bullets, guns, tanks, planes and battleships that are used, lost or destroyed have to be constantly replaced. It is very difficult to put a price on how much a war has cost, but many people have tried it. US President Harry S. Truman claimed in 1948 that the USA had spent around $341 billion on World War Two (around £2100 billion in today's money). It is said that Britain's total spend on World War Two in today's money was around £600 billion. Britain got into massive debt as a result and only managed to finish paying off the loans in 2006. The money Britain borrowed from the USA to fight World War One (about £40 billion) has still not been repaid! Source B tries to put the cost of World War Two into perspective.

The human cost of war

Perhaps the most important cost of any war is the human cost. War not only affects soldiers, sailors and airmen but also their families and all the ordinary civilians living in the countries involved. In World War Two, for example, more civilians died than soldiers. IIn more recent conflicts, civilian deaths have remained very high. In the Vietnam War (1955–1975), for example, around 1,000,000 civilians died, and the Iraq War (which began in 2003) has seen around 100,000 civilian casualties. In addition, Source E shows that casualties of war cannot just be counted in terms of deaths and physical injuries – the psychological cost of war must be taken into account too.

↵ **SOURCE B:** *The cost of World War Two.*

UK's £20 billion bill for fighting Iraq and Afghan Wars

Fighting the wars in Afghanistan and Iraq alongside the US has cost British taxpayers more than £20 billion since 2001, it emerged yesterday.

The bill includes £18 billion for military operations as well as paying for overseas development and aid. However, the £20.34 billion total does not include the salaries of soldiers or paying for their long term injuries and mental health care.

It is also on top of the £35 billion annual defence budget.

↳ **SOURCE C:** *From a* Daily Mail *article, June 2010.*

Work

1 Why do wars cost such a lot of money?

2 Why do you think that some countries choose to spend so much on their armed forces?

3 Why do you think some people believe spending large amounts of money on weapons is wrong?

4 Look at Source A.
   a What countries are the key weapon-making nations, according to this source?
   b Can you think of advantages and disadvantages to being a key weapon-making country?

5 What is meant by the term 'the human cost of war'?

THESE ARE WHAT THE MONEY SPENT BY BRITAIN ON THE WAR WOULD HAVE BOUGHT (AT 1940 PRICES)

| 2 NEW HOUSES AND 2 NEW CARS FOR EVERY FAMILY IN BRITAIN | 100 000 NEW SCHOOLS AND 100 000 NEW HOSPITALS | A MOTORWAY TWICE AROUND THE WORLD | A DECENT STANDARD OF LIVING FOR EVERYONE IN THE WORLD. |

BRITAIN'S WAR BILL £ 40 000 000 000

INSTEAD IT WAS SPENT ON TANKS, SHIPS, PLANES, BOMBS, SOLDIERS, SAILORS AND AIRMEN

| GERMANY'S WAR BILL WAS MORE THAN TWICE THE SIZE OF BRITAIN'S | AMERICA'S WAR BILL WAS MORE THAN THREE TIMES THE SIZE OF BRITAIN'S | THE TOTAL COST OF THE WAR HAS BEEN ESTIMATED AT £ 390 000 000 000 |

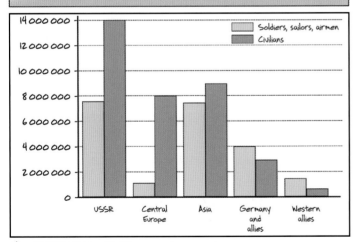

↳ **SOURCE D:** *Civilian and armed forces casualties from World War Two. The eight million casualties in Central Europe (Poland, Hungary etc.) were mainly Jews murdered by the Nazis. 9 million Asian civilians (mainly Chinese) were caught up in the conflict between Japan and China.*

'The true cost of the war will become clear only in the decades to come when troops suffering from long term mental and physical injuries seek treatment.'

↵ **SOURCE E:** *Professor Malcolm Chambers, a defence expert speaking in a* Daily Mail Online *article (21 June 2010) about recent wars in Iraq and Afghanistan.*

—MISSION ACCOMPLISHED?—

- Are you able to outline how wars involve a variety of 'costs', not just the amount of money a government has to pay?

Will there ever be a World War Three?

————————— MISSION OBJECTIVES —————————
- To understand how the United Nations tries to prevent war.
- To remember two instances where nuclear war nearly happened.

On 27 October 1962 a Russian submarine, armed with nuclear weapons, was tracked by US Navy warships near Cuba. The ships began dropping practice **depth charges** on it. These are explosives designed to make a lot of noise and force submarines to the surface. The Russian captain wanted to launch a nuclear-tipped torpedo at the US ships, but needed two of the other officers on board to agree. There is little doubt that if they had, the USA would **have retaliated**… and a *nuclear war* would have begun! But one of the three, Vasili Arkhipov, was against the attack, so the torpedo wasn't fired and war was avoided. Years later, a US politician said that World War Three would have broken out that day, but 'a guy called Vasili Arkhipov saved the world'. Most historians agree that this crisis in 1962 was the point at which the risk of World War Three was greatest. But at what other points in history have we been close to World War Three? How was it avoided? And will there ever be a World War Three?

What is World War Three?
World War Three (also called the Third World War or WWIII) is the **hypothetical** successor to the two World Wars that took place between 1914–1918 and 1939–1949. It is often suggested that any future World War would be fought with nuclear weapons and be very, very destructive!

Millions died during World War One, and millions more died during World War Two. As a result, great effort has gone into making sure that every possible precaution is taken to avoid a World War Three. One of the most important forces in this is a group called the United Nations.

'If the third World War is fought with nuclear weapons, the fourth will be fought with bows and arrows.'

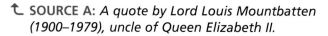

↳ **SOURCE A:** *A quote by Lord Louis Mountbatten (1900–1979), uncle of Queen Elizabeth II.*

↳ **SOURCE B:** *The fiery mushroom cloud that follows the detonation of a nuclear bomb. This test explosion took place in 1953.*

What is the United Nations?

Towards the end of World War Two a new group was set up to work towards long-term world peace. They wanted fewer weapons in the world, better healthcare for everyone and peaceful solutions to arguments between nations. Called the United Nations Organisation (or **UN** for short) the group today contains the vast majority of the world's countries. Representatives from these nations meet regularly and have had many successes in preventing war and improving the world. There have also been failures – but most people agree that the UN is a peaceful, well-meaning organisation that has had a positive effect on the world.

So how close have we been to World War Three?

There have been a number of times when the world held its breath and waited for World War Three to start, but it has never happened!

- In 1956, a war between Britain, France, Israel and Egypt (the Suez Crisis) threatened to turn into a much bigger conflict. At one point a senior Russian politician warned the British that 'if this war isn't stopped soon it carries the danger of turning into a third world war'.

- In 1962, tension grew between the USA and Russia over Russian nuclear missile bases in Cuba, to the point where a leading US politician said that he feared he 'might never live to see another Saturday night'. Thankfully, the UN helped sort out an agreement between the US and Russia that avoided nuclear war. It was during this Cuban missile crisis that Vasili Arkhipov refused to launch nuclear missiles at US ships.

- In 1983, a nuclear attack early warning station detected five US nuclear missiles heading for Russia. A Russian army colonel, Stanislav Petrov, correctly worked out that it was a false alarm caused by faulty machinery. If he hadn't, the Russians were set to fire missiles back. Petrov has been called 'the man who saved the world'.

Is World War Three ever going to happen?

World War Three has been the theme of Hollywood movies, video games and novels. It is a common topic for TV and radio shows, websites, newspapers and classrooms. Much of the discussion centres around whether World War Three will ever happen, and the answer is always the same… who knows? On the one hand, it can be argued that organizations like the UN work so hard to prevent conflict that a World War would never be allowed to happen again. However, there is a fear that one small incident, which may seem insignificant at the time, could start off a chain of events that drags the world's most powerful nations into all-out war.

What is the Doomsday Clock?

The Doomsday Clock is a symbolic clock that nuclear scientists use to show how close they think the world is to global nuclear war. The closer to midnight, the closer the world is to disaster. Since it was set up in 1947, the time on the clock has changed around 20 times. The closest it has been to midnight was in 1953 (11:58pm) when the USA and Russia both tested the world's largest nuclear bomb within months of each other (see Source B). It also got very close in the 1960s and early 1980s, and in 2002, concerns about terrorist groups getting hold of nuclear weapons led the scientists to move the time again. Why not find out how close some of the world's most gifted scientists think the world is to disaster today?

WISE-UP Words

depth charges

hypothetical

retaliated

UN

Work

1 **a** What is meant by the term 'World War Three'?
  b Explain how World War Three nearly broke out in:
   1956   1962   1983

2 Look at Source A. What point is being made here?

3 What is the UN?

4 'Nuclear weapons are both a threat and a deterrent'. What do you think this statement means?

5 **a** What is the Doomsday Clock?
  b When was the clock closest to midnight?
  c Do you think the clock is useful or not? Explain your answer in detail.

⤴ SOURCE C: *Doomsday Clock, based in Chicago, USA.*

MISSION ACCOMPLISHED?

- Could you explain to a friend how the United Nations works?

Have you been learning? 2

TASK 1 What about war?

Read carefully through the following quotes. You might want to discuss them with a partner or in a small group. Then try to agree on where you would place them on the 'continuum line' (you might want to draw your own one of these on a piece of paper or in your book).

Continuum line

←——————————————————————→

Completely agree   Completely disagree

A: 'In war there are no unwounded soldiers' – Jose Narosky

B: 'You can no more win a war than you can win an earthquake' – Jeanette Rankin

C: 'If we do not end war, war will end us. Everybody says that, millions of people believe it, and nobody does anything' – H. G. Wells

D: 'All wars are civil wars, because all men are brothers' – François Fenelon

E: 'Why do we kill people who are killing people to show that killing people is wrong?' – Holly Near

F: 'It seems like such a terrible shame that innocent civilians have to get hurt in wars, otherwise combat would be such a wonderfully healthy way to rid the human race of unneeded trash' – Fred Woodworth

G: 'Never think that war, no matter how necessary, nor how justified, is not a crime' – Ernest Hemingway

H: 'They wrote in the old days that it is sweet and fitting to die for one's country. But in modern war there is nothing fitting in your dying. You will die like a dog for no good reason' – Ernest Hemingway

TASK 2 The United Nations: Preventing war in today's world

Towards the end of World War Two, Britain, Russia and the USA realized they had to prevent such a war ever happening again. They knew that developments in science and technology (like nuclear weapons) would make future wars even more deadly. They believed that if there was more cooperation between countries, they could come together to discuss problems without having to resort to war. So they set up a group for all the world's nations – called the United Nations (UN) – which meets to sort out international problems. The UN also has special organizations to deal with world issues such as health and child poverty. Source A sums up the work of the UN today.

SOURCE A:

Security Council

The five most powerful countries at the end of World War II (Britain, France, the USA, Russia and China) formed the permanent **Security Council**. They were joined by ten other countries (temporary members) and meet when it looks like a dispute could turn into a war. They can stop countries attacking each other by:

- asking all UN members to stop trading with them until a shortage of supplies forces them to back away from war
- sending in soldiers – or peacekeepers – to prevent or contain the fighting.

Any decisions need a 'yes' from all five permanent members and peacekeepers are sent from armies of several countries.

World Health Organization (WHO)

Mounts health campaigns, does research, runs clinics and vaccinates against infectious diseases.

The General Assembly

A sort of world Parliament, with each country having one vote. There were 51 member countries in 1945. By 2000 there were 184.

Secretary General

A key person who manages the UN and speaks on its behalf.

International Labour Organization (ILO)

Tries to protect workers all over the world by improving their conditions, pay, rights and insurance.

Children's fund (UNICEF)

Helps underfed, poorly treated or neglected children throughout the world.

International Court of Justice

Based in Holland. Fifteen judges, each from a different nation, settle legal disputes between countries before they lead to war.

Educational, Scientific and Cultural Organization (UNESCO)

Tries to get countries to share each other's films, books, music, sport and scientific discoveries so that they understand each other more and are less likely to fight.

'United Nations armies have fought in Korea, Cyprus and the Congo, and in these three alone have prevented what could easily have developed into World War III. Another important committee [of the UN] is the International Court of Justice which meets in Holland. Fifteen judges, each one from a different nation, sit to settle points of law which arise between countries which could lead to war.'

↳ **SOURCE B:** *From* History Alive *by Peter Moss (Hart Davis, 1978)*

There were many crises in world affairs where the United Nations did not act either because the Security Council and General Assembly could not agree about what should be done, or because the great powers simply ignored them. The United Nations took no active part in the rebellion in Hungary (1956), the Cuban crisis of 1962, the Vietnam War (1964–8), the Russian invasion of Afghanistan (1979) or the Falklands War (1982). Nor have all interventions been successful. The UN originally became involved in former Yugoslavia as a peacekeeping force; by 1995 the UN forces had themselves become part of the problem as the warring sides ignored them.'

↳ **SOURCE C:** *From* The Modern World *by Nigel Kelly and Rosemary Rees (Heinemann, 1996)*

a Why was the UN set up?
b In your own words, describe the role of the UN in the modern world.
c Look at Sources B and C. Explain what each source is saying about the UN.
d Can you explain why there are always so many different opinions in history, even when people are writing about the same thing?

Glossary

antibiotic a drug used to treat infections by killing bacteria

artillery large weapons, such as guns and cannons, that fire over long distances

atl-atl a prehistoric device used to help a person throw their spear further

attrition to wear away gradually

battering ram a huge machine used to break down walls or gates

battle a fight between two opposing armies in a specific place

blitzkrieg a military tactic used by the Germans in the Second World War, where all military power was concentrated together

bombard an early type of cannon that fired iron balls

caltrop an iron spike put on the ground to stab feet

catapult a machine for hurling stones and other missiles

cauterize burn the flesh of a wound to seal the blood vessels and stop bleeding

cavalry soldiers who fight on horseback

chariot a two-wheeled horsedrawn vehicle

civil war war between different groups of the same country

conscription making it compulsory for all men of a certain age to fight, if called up

depth charges explosives dropped under water to attack submarines

diphtheria an infectious disease of the nose, throat and air passages

evacuated to be sent to a safer area to avoid the effects of war

frizzen an L-shaped piece of metal used in guns

graft surgically attach

handgun a small gun that can be held in one hand

home front the civilians at home during a war while armed forces are fighting abroad

hypothetical an idea that is unproven

Iceni a British tribe inhabiting an area of south east Britain in the early CE centuries

infantry soldiers who fight on foot

knight a highly trained armour-wearing warrior of 'noble birth'

marines troops who serve in the navy

mobilize to prepare, put into operation

musket an early type of rifle (long gun)

Mutually Assured Destruction (MAD) a policy acknowledging that if two opposing sides use nuclear warfare against each other, both sides will be destroyed

pacifist someone who does not believe in war at any cost

paratroopers soldiers trained to parachute from aircraft

rationing limiting of food, clothing and fuel by the government

resistance groups groups of people who fight against an invader in their country

retaliated attacked back

rifle a long gun designed to be fired from the shoulder

rifling a pattern of grooves in a rifle barrel, designed to make bullets spin when fired

rocket a fast-moving weapon propelled by engines

sabotage deliberately damage

seaman someone who serves in the navy

sever cut off

siege when enemy forces surround a castle or city trying to get in, while the people inside try to keep them out

snipers marksmen who shoot targets from a great distance

theatres of war areas where fighting takes place

total war where the entire country armed forces and civilians are involved in the war

tourniquet material tied tightly round a wounded limb to cut off blood circulation and stop bleeding

transfusion the process of replacing blood

UN United Nations an organisation set up to work towards long-term world peace

war the act of fighting between two or more groups, nations or countries

warfare the tactics, methods, strategies and fighting used in war

weapon an item used to harm, kill or destroy

weaponry the invention and production of weapons

Zeppelins huge German inflatable airships used for bombing during the World Wars

Index